WRITE SOURCE

Inside Writing Skills

Instruction and Practice

. . . a resource of student activities
to accompany

Inside Writing

WRITE SOURCE®

GREAT SOURCE EDUCATION GROUP

a division of Houghton Mifflin Company
Wilmington, Massachusetts

A Few Words About
Inside Writing Skills

Before you begin . . .

   Inside Writing Skills provides you with opportunities to practice the editing and proofreading skills presented in the *Inside Writing* units.

Activities

   Each skills activity includes a brief introduction to the topic and examples showing how to complete the activity. The first section, "Proofreading Activities," focuses on punctuation, on the mechanics of writing, and on usage. The second section, "Sentence Activities," provides practice in sentence combining and in correcting common sentence problems. The third section addresses the parts of speech. Many exercises include a Next Step activity that provides follow-up work, often in the form of a brief writing assignment.

Proofreader's Guide

   The "Proofreader's Guide" (pages 139-183) presents the basic rules for punctuation, capitalization, spelling, and grammar. Activities are cross-referenced to the information in this part of the book to help you complete your work. You can also turn to this guide whenever you have an editing or proofreading question when you write.

Authors: Pat Sebranek and Dave Kemper

Printed in the United States of America

International Standard Book Number: 978-0-669-50811-6 (student edition)

3 4 5 6 7 8 9 10 -POO- 10 09 08 07

International Standard Book Number: 0-669-50812-8 (teacher's edition)

1 2 3 4 5 6 7 8 9 10 -POO- 10 09 08 07 06 05 04 03

Inside Writing SKILLS

Proofreading Activities

Marking Punctuation

Editing for Mechanics

Using the Right Word

Sentence Activities

Understanding Sentences

Sentence Problems

Sentence Combining

Parts of Speech Activities

Nouns

Pronouns

Verbs

Adjectives and Adverbs

Interjections, Prepositions, and Conjunctions

Proofreader's Guide

Turn to this section to find information to help with each of the skills activities. You will find page numbers for the "Proofreader's Guide" in the upper right-hand corner of each exercise. You may also use this handy reference to find answers when you have questions about punctuation and grammar in your own writing.

Proofreading Activities

The activities in this section include sentences that need to be checked for punctuation, mechanics, and correct word choice. For more information and examples, all of the activities include page references to the "Proofreader's Guide." In addition, the **Next Step** activities encourage follow-up practice of certain skills.

1

End Punctuation

At the end of a sentence, use a **period**, a **question mark**, or an **exclamation point**.

Examples

Egypt's pyramids are ancient. (period)
How many pyramids are there? (question mark)
There aren't very many! (exclamation point)

> **Directions** >> **Add end punctuation to the following sentences. The first sentence has been done for you.**

1. The Pyramids were built more than 4,000 years ago.

2. They were giant tombs for Egypt's kings and queens.

3. Do you know where the three most famous pyramids are located?

4. They are along the Nile River in Giza, Egypt.

5. How long does it take to walk around the Great Pyramid?

6. It's a 15-minute walk.

7. That pyramid must be enormous!

8. Egyptians worked more than 50 years to build it.

9. What is the Sphinx?

10. It's a huge stone sculpture of a lion with a human head.

11. Wasn't it supposed to guard the Pyramids and the Nile River?

12. That's right!

Add a period, a question mark, or an exclamation point to the following sentences. The first one has been done for you.

1. My dad came up with a great idea.

2. What was it

3. He said we should have a dessert dinner

4. What an excellent idea

5. All of us voted, and Dad counted the votes

6. Which dessert won

7. Ice-cream sundaes got the most votes

8. Great, I love ice-cream sundaes, too

9. I asked Dad if we could do this again tomorrow

10. What did he say

11. He said tomorrow night's dinner would be all vegetables

Write a few sentences about your dinner. Use end punctuation correctly.

....

....

....

Commas in a Series

Use **commas** between words or phrases in a series.

Examples

Cub Scouts learn to be **trustworthy, loyal,** and **kind.** (words in a series)

Their leaders teach Scouts **to respect themselves, to work together,** and **to honor the flag.** (phrases in a series)

> **Directions** ⟫ Add commas to separate words or phrases in a series in the following sentences. The first one has been done for you.

1. Paul∧Alex∧and Collin are Cub Scouts.

2. There are Cub Scouts in almost every city, town, and rural area of the United States.

3. Boy Scouts can be found in Turkey, Liberia, Thailand, and Bolivia.

4. Cub Scouts learn to be good citizens, get along with others, and have fun.

5. Scout law teaches Scouts to be courteous, helpful, friendly, thrifty, cheerful, and brave.

6. Swimming, cooking, and woodworking are some of the skills the Scouts learn.

7. This summer the Scouts hiked around the boundary of their city, went camping in the north woods, and learned how to tie three different kinds of knots.

Add commas between items in a series in this telephone message. The first sentence has been done for you.

1   This afternoon I wrote down messages from Uncle Jason,

2   Mrs. Chang, and Luke. The calls came in at 10:00 A.M.

3   2:30 P.M. and 5:00 P.M. Uncle Jason said he would buy tickets

4   pack his cooler and drive his car to the baseball game next

5   weekend. Mrs. Chang told me that she needs my homework

6   field-trip money and permission slip by Friday. She said my

7   math science and reading groups miss me. Then Luke called to

8   ask Mom if she would order popcorn sell raffle tickets and work

9   for an hour at his fund-raiser.

Choose one of the lists below. Write a sentence using that list. Use commas between the items in a series.

puppy	milk	bike	jumping
kitten	flour	scooter	fishing
guppy	eggs	tricycle	soccer

Commas in Dates and Addresses

Play ball!

Use **commas** to separate items in dates and addresses.

Examples

On April 18, 1923, the Yankees and Boston Red Sox played the first game in the New Yankee Stadium in New York, New York.
(When an address or a date is at the beginning or in the middle of the sentence, add a comma right after it.)

Directions ▶ Add commas where needed in the following sentences. The first one has been done for you.

1. On June 10, 1944, a 15-year-old pitched for the Cincinnati Reds.

2. The National Baseball Hall of Fame is in Cooperstown, New York.

3. Fenway Park in Boston, Massachusetts was built in 1912.

4. Wrigley Field in Chicago, Illinois is one of the oldest ballparks.

5. The first game at Wrigley Field was played on April 23, 1914.

6. On October 7, 2001 Barry Bonds hit his 73rd home run.

7. I watched on TV from my home at 1901 Wickley Drive Bronson, North Carolina.

NEXT STEP

Write a sentence using your birthday and your address.

....

....

Commas in Compound Sentences

A **comma** is used right before a coordinating conjunction to connect two simple sentences. This forms a compound sentence. Coordinating conjunctions are words such as *and, but, or, so, for,* and *yet.*

Example

We play in our tree house, **but** we don't live in it.

Directions > Add commas to the compound sentences in the story that follows. The first sentence has been done for you.

1 The barn rafters creaked, and James stopped milking. The

2 beams overhead shuddered with the storm, and wind whistled

3 through the roof. The cow in front of James shivered, for she

4 knew something was wrong.

5 "It's a scary storm, yet I will keep you safe, Old Bess."

6 Her hooves thumped the dirt floor, but she was tied in the

7 stall. Suddenly the barn shook, and the windows exploded.

8 "We've got to get out of here, or we're done for!" James

9 released Old Bess, and she bounded out the barn doors.

10 Then James saw the twister, and he dived into a ditch. The

11 whole barn collapsed sideways. From the ditch, James called,

12 "Thanks, Old Bess, for you're the one who kept me safe."

Commas with Phrases

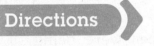

Use a **comma** to set off a long phrase that comes before the main part of a sentence.

Example

After a few tries and sputters, the engine finally fired up.

> **Directions** ⟫ Add a comma to separate the long phrase from the main part in each of the following sentences. The first one has been done for you.

1. In my great-grandmother's time, chairs often had legs shaped like animal legs.

2. To make the first hairbrushes, people used hog hair.

3. Invented for a king in France, the first elevator was called the Flying Chair.

4. Unfortunately for the first gum chewers, the first chewing gum had no flavor.

5. Without the safety pin, our world might fall apart!

6. Before the invention of color TV, all television programs were filmed in black and white.

7. Introduced to the public in the late 1890s, zippers were originally used to zip and unzip shoes.

8. Thanks to many inventors, America is the "invention capital" of the world.

1   According to Chinese legend∧silk was discovered long, long

2   ago. Like many other discoveries this one wasn't planned. In the

3   Emperor Huanghis' beautiful garden something awful was going

4   on. For some strange reason the mulberry trees were being

5   destroyed. Upset by the damage to his favorite trees the emperor

6   sent his wife, Xiling Shi, to investigate. To her great surprise

7   she found white worms eating the leaves and spinning cocoons.

8   Xiling Shi pulled a branch down and picked one of the cocoons

9   from the tree. Later, while looking at the cocoon she accidentally

10   dropped it into her cup of tea. Surrounded by hot tea the cocoon

11   began to unravel. While picking up the cocoon Xiling Shi found

12   a long, white thread. The Chinese silk industry was born.

NEXT STEP What new invention would you like to see? Describe it in two or three sentences. Use some long introductory phrases and use commas correctly.

....

....

....

Commas to Set Off Clauses

Commas can also be used to set off a long clause. A clause is a group of words that has both a subject and a predicate. Dependent clauses usually begin with a word called a *subordinating conjunction*.

Example

Although you may be awake or asleep, your muscles are working.
(The subordinating conjunction "although" starts this clause, and a comma sets it off from the rest of the sentence.)

Directions ▶ Each sentence below starts with a long clause. Add a comma after each clause. The first one has been done for you.

1. If you didn't have muscles, you couldn't sit, run, swim, or throw a ball.

2. When you smile or wiggle your ears, you use muscles.

3. While some muscles rest, others never stop.

4. As long as you're alive, your heart—a muscle—works.

5. After you swallow food, your stomach muscles go to work.

6. Even when you're asleep, your breathing muscles are wide awake.

7. Before certain muscles will move, you must send a signal from your brain.

8. Though some muscles must wait for the brain's command, others don't need to be "told" to move.

Finish the following sentences. Remember to add a comma after each clause and punctuate the end of the sentence.

1. Unless I exercise ....

....

2. When I was in fourth grade ....

....

3. After we left school on Friday ....

....

4. While I watch TV ....

....

5. If I could eat anything for breakfast ....

....

6. Since _____ is older than I am ....
   (your choice of a noun)

....

Write two of your own sentences about friends. Use long introductory clauses in each sentence.

....

....

....

Comma Review

This activity reviews ways to use commas.

> **Directions** ⟩⟩ Add commas where needed in compound sentences and in series of words.

1. Do you know the planets and can you name them in order?

2. Mercury Venus Earth Mars Jupiter Saturn Uranus Neptune and Pluto are the nine planets.

3. Neptune has eleven moons yet Earth has only one.

4. Mars has the largest canyon and it has the highest volcano.

5. Venus is covered with craters mountains and volcanoes.

> **Directions** ⟩⟩ Now add commas in dates, in addresses, and after long introductory phrases and clauses.

1. Because Jupiter is so large the other eight planets could fit inside it.

2. Besides the sun and moon Venus shines the brightest in our sky.

3. Because of its color Mars is called the Red Planet.

4. Pluto was seen from an observatory in Flagstaff Arizona in 1930.

5. On October 4 1957 the first satellite, *Sputnik*, was launched into space.

6. On July 20 1969 the first humans landed on the moon's surface.

1   On December 24 1968 *Apollo 8* was circling the moon.

2 Astronauts Borman Lovell and Anders were on board. Though

3 they were 240,000 miles from Earth their broadcasts were being

4 followed around the world. They had finished their work but

5 they had one last surprise for earthlings. As they began their

6 broadcast each man took a turn speaking. They described what

7 they had seen felt and thought on their incredible journey. They

8 pointed their camera toward the moon. In the distance, the

9 beautiful, blue marble called Earth was rising in the sky. People

10 on Earth gasped in wonder excitement and awe for no one had

11 ever seen Earth this way before.

Colons

Use a **colon** between the hours and minutes in time. Also use a colon to introduce a list. (Don't forget to add commas to a list that follows a colon.)

Examples

3:45 A.M.   9:00 P.M.

My snack choices are the following: popcorn, fruit, or cereal bars.

Directions ⟩ **Add colons and commas to the following sentences. The first one has been done for you.**

1. I make lunch at 11:30 on Saturdays.

2. For sandwiches, I need the following bread peanut butter and jelly.

3. I also make salads with these fruits grapes apples melons bananas and strawberries.

4. At 100 I ride my bike to my piano lesson.

5. I pass the following streets Bell Woodland and Franklin.

6. After my lesson, my piano teacher often gives me one of these treats cookies brownies or cake.

7. I stop at the library at 230.

8. I look at the following magazines *National Geographic for Kids Ranger Rick* and *Time for Kids*.

9. By 500 I am on my way home.

Hyphens

Use **hyphens** to divide words when there isn't room for the whole word on the line. Words should be divided only between syllables. One-syllable words are never divided.

Example

This morning, we looked everywhere for the **missing** jacket.

> **Directions** ⟩⟩ Write each word on the line, dividing it into syllables with hyphens. Use a dictionary if you are unsure of how to divide a word. If a word cannot be divided, write "NO" on the line. The first one has been done for you.

1. program   *pro-gram*   5. caught   _____

2. showed   _____   6. divide   _____

3. hobby   _____   7. direction   _____

4. professional   _____   8. understand   _____

Use a hyphen to join two words that form a single adjective and come before a noun.

Examples

my **fun-loving** brother   her **worn-out** jeans

> **Directions** ⟩⟩ Put hyphens where they are needed in these sentences. The first one has been done for you.

1. My dad makes many long-distance calls.

2. This old fashioned Valentine is pretty.

3. My sister bought some fat free cookies.

4. I like ice cream sandwiches.

Punctuating Titles

Underline the titles of books, newspapers, magazines, TV programs, and movies. Use quotation marks for titles of poems, songs, short stories, and chapters.

Examples

<u>A Girl Named Disaster</u> (book title)

"The Walrus and the Carpenter" (poem)

Directions Underline or add quotation marks to the titles in the following sentences. The first one has been done for you.

1. <u>Whale Rider</u> is a movie about a gutsy girl in New Zealand.

2. "Fog" is a famous poem by Carl Sandburg.

3. Three of Walter Dean Myers' greatest books are <u>Fallen Angels,</u> <u>Hoops,</u> and <u>Scorpions.</u>

4. <u>Boys' Life</u> and <u>American Girl</u> are two children's magazines.

5. In my history book, I'm reading a chapter called "East Meets West."

6. <u>The Great Fire</u> by Jim Murphy is a book about the terrible 1871 Chicago fire.

7. Alma Flor Ada's short story, "The Gold Coin," is about farm workers.

8. <u>Wheel of Fortune</u> is my grandpa's favorite TV show.

9. Should "America the Beautiful" be our national anthem?

Apostrophes 1

Use an **apostrophe** to show that one or more letters have been left out of a word to form a contraction.

Examples

would not — **wouldn't**   I have — **I've**   you will — **you'll**

Directions ▷ Write a contraction for every word pair below. The first one has been done for you.

1. I am .... *I'm* ....
2. she is ....
3. they are ....
4. there is ....
5. does not ....
6. will not ....
7. has not ....
8. he will ....
9. they will ....
10. should not ....

11. it is ....
12. we have ....
13. do not ....
14. is not ....
15. they have ....
16. you are ....
17. can not ....
18. are not ....
19. would have ....
20. let us ....

Write a sentence that uses as many contractions as possible. Share your sentence with the class.

....

....

Apostrophes 2

Apostrophes are added to nouns to show ownership. These nouns are called possessive nouns.

Singular Possessive Nouns

cook's apron (Add an apostrophe plus an "s" to most singular nouns to make them possessive.)

Thomas' turtle (When a singular noun ends with an "s" or "z" sound, the possessive may be formed by adding just an apostrophe.)

Plural Possessive Nouns

players' scores (Add only an apostrophe after a plural noun ending in an "s.")

children's petting zoo (If the plural does not end in "s," add an apostrophe plus an "s.")

> **Directions** ▶ On each line, write the possessive of the noun in parentheses. The first one has been done for you.

1. We found a _____*bird's*_____ *(bird)* nest on the ground.

2. The gerbils stay in the _____ *(boys)* room.

3. A _____ *(tree)* bark is its skin.

4. _____ *(Gita)* father is from India.

5. All the _____ *(men)* clothing was on sale.

6. Angie is coaching the _____ *(girls)* soccer team.

7. _____ *(Ben)* picture won first prize.

8. We saw the _____ *(monkeys)* tails around the branches.

9. This _____ *(year)* temperatures are above normal.

10. The _____ *(babies)* bottles got all mixed up.

1. The assembly is held in our ___school's___ (school) gym.

2. All of the _____ (students) names are on the class lists.

3. Rosa is in _____ (Ms. Alton) class this year.

4. As we walk to our classroom, _____ (Jon) brother tells us about the mystery pet.

5. _____ (Mr. Rivers) class gets a new class pet each year.

6. We go into the classroom and find the mystery _____ (pet) cage is open.

7. Fortunately, our _____ (room) new pet did not escape.

8. It is crouching in a basket on _____ (Tonya) desk.

9. A white _____ (rabbit) pink eyes stare up at us.

10. It will be the _____ (volunteers) job to take care of the class rabbit.

11. When Mr. Rivers asks for volunteers, _____ (everyone) hand goes up.

Apostrophe Review

This activity reviews apostrophes used in contractions and possessive nouns.

> **Directions** >> On each line, write the contraction (C) or possessive form (P) of the words in parentheses.

1. _____ (P—*Wilma Mankiller*) ancestors were Cherokee.

2. She grew up on _____ (P—*Oklahoma*) tribal lands.

3. Her _____ (P—*family*) life changed when they were forced to move to California.

4. As an adult, Wilma learned about the _____ (P—*government*) unfair treatment of Native Americans.

5. She moved back to Oklahoma because she wanted to improve the

   Native American _____ (P—*people*) lives.

6. She was hurt in a car accident, but she _____ (C—*did not*) die.

7. She _____ (C—*could not*) walk for a long time.

8. Her _____ (P—*brother*) transplanted kidney saved her life.

9. But Wilma _____ (C—*would not*) let her own problems stop her work for the Cherokee people.

10. She decided to run for the _____ (P—*chief*) position in her tribe.

11. That _____ (C—*was not*) a popular idea with some people.

12. Wilma Mankiller became the _____ (P—*nation*) only woman to lead a major Native American tribe.

Add apostrophes where needed in the following paragraph. (There are five.) Above each underlined pair of words, write its contraction.

1   These people survived war, famine, poverty, and a long

2   march across this country called "The Trail of Tears." <u>They are</u>

3   the Cherokee, the largest Native American tribe in the United

4   States. In the 1800s, the Cherokee people <u>were not</u> poor. They

5   were one of this countrys richest tribes. It <u>was not</u> long after

6   the white settlers arrival that the Cherokee were forced out of

7   their native land. The Trail of Tears in the winter of 1838-39

8   <u>should not</u> have happened. The childrens cries filled the air. The

9   womens and mens pleas were ignored. Fifteen thousand Cherokee

10   people were marched from North Carolina to Oklahoma.

11   Thousands <u>did not</u> make it. Today, the Cherokee <u>have not</u>

12   forgotten their history and culture.

Punctuating Dialogue

Dialogue is talk between two people. In writing, spoken words appear with quotation marks around them. Use commas to separate dialogue from the rest of the sentence. (Periods and commas at the end of a quotation always go inside the quotation marks.)

Examples

Juan asked, "Who was Aesop?"
(The speaker is named at the beginning of the sentence.)

"We can't be sure," said Mr. Martinez. "Many people think he was Greek."
(The speaker is named in the middle of the sentence.)

"Whoever he was, he told great stories," said Juan.
(The speaker is named at the end of the sentence.)

 **Directions** Add commas and quotation marks where needed in the following sentences. The first sentence has been done for you.

1. "Look what I've found," said a man walking down a road. "It's a bag filled with gold."

2. The second man said, "You should share it with me."

3. "No," said the first man. "I found it, and I shall keep it all."

4. Just then a voice shouted, "Stop, thief!"

5. "We are in terrible trouble," said the first man.

6. "What do you mean 'we' are in trouble?" asked the second man.

7. "You didn't want to share your good luck, so I don't plan to share your bad luck."

The Three Wishes—
A Folktale from Puerto Rico

1   "Give me food," the beggar whispered. "I am weak with

2   hunger."

3   "Come in," replied the woman. "I am poor, but I will gladly

4   share my bread with you."

5   When he had eaten his fill, the beggar said, "Because you

6   treated me well, you may have three wishes."

7   "Oh, I wish my husband were here to see this!" she

8   exclaimed. In an instant, her husband appeared.

9   When he heard about the wishes, the husband complained,

10 "You have wasted a precious wish. I wish you had donkey ears."

11 "Oh no!" she cried, as she felt her ears begin to grow.

12 The beggar, who was watching all this from a corner, said,

13 "You have one wish left. Think carefully, my friends."

14 The husband looked at his miserable wife and said, "May we

15 be as happy as we once were." Instantly, the donkey ears

16 disappeared, and the couple smiled.

17 The beggar said, "You have chosen wisely."

Punctuation Review

This activity reviews punctuation you have learned.

Directions ❯ Add end punctuation, commas, and underlining where they're needed in the following paragraph.

1   Do you have to go to the country to see wildlife Absolutely

2   not Towns cities and suburbs are filled with wildlife On June 20

3   2003 the Kansas City Star newspaper ran an article about

4   backyard wildlife Deer, it seems, have moved to the suburbs

5   Even animals like foxes coyotes and porcupines have been

6   spotted in cities and suburbs

Directions ❯ Continue making punctuation corrections. This time focus on adding commas, quotation marks, and apostrophes. You will also need to add two hyphens and a colon.

1   If you leave your trash uncovered you may have visits from

2   one of the following black masked raccoons gray squirrels or

3   white nosed opossums. They will think youre inviting them to a

4   neighborhood block party. Like other partygoers theyll leave you

5   with a mess to clean up in the morning.

6   Its a jungle out there said our neighbor, Mr. Fisher, and he

7   wasnt talking about the Amazon.

Directions Read the paragraphs below. As you add punctuation, put a check next to the type of correction.

Paragraph 1
comma ___ ___ ___ ___   apostrophe ___
end punctuation ___ ___ ___ ___ ___   colon ___

1   Attention all couch potatoes Its time to start moving

2   There are lots of ways to get enough exercise and most of

3   them are fun You can choose from one or more of the

4   following sports softball basketball football or soccer Remember

5   that you don't have to be the star of the team Just start

6   exercising each day.

Paragraph 2
comma ___ ___ ___ ___   apostrophe ___
end punctuation ___ ___ ___   quotation marks ___ ___

7   If you say that sports arent for you then find other ways

8   to get exercise Ride your bike swim a few laps or jog a mile

9   The easiest way to get going is to follow the words of President

10 Thomas Jefferson. He said Walking is the best possible exercise

Paragraph 3
end punctuation ___ ___ ___   comma ___ ___ ___ ___

11   Begin now Your muscles will grow stronger you will look

12 healthier and you will have more energy Get up off the couch

13 take a walk outside and start down the road to good health

Capital Letters 1

Capitalize the first word in a sentence or a quotation.

Order!
Order!
Order!

Examples

The mouse said, "This meeting is called to order."

Directions >> In the following sentences, cross out any letter that should be capitalized. Write the capital letter above it. The first one has been done for you.

1. *L*
   ~~L~~ong ago the mice were having a convention.

2. one asked, "what shall we do to protect ourselves from the cat?"

3. a brainy mouse said, "i have an idea."

4. "what is it?" asked the other mice.

5. the brainy mouse said, "we should hang a bell around the cat's neck

   to warn us when she is around."

6. "what a brilliant idea!" said one mouse.

7. everyone was excited by this solution to a longtime problem.

8. then a wise, old mouse rose from his chair to speak.

9. "that is fine," he said, "but who will put the bell on the cat?"

NEXT STEP

Write a couple more sentences of dialogue between two mice who have a plan for getting the bell around the cat's neck.

....

....

Capital Letters 2

Capitalize all proper nouns. A proper noun names a specific person, place, thing, or idea.

Examples

Valentina Tereshkova, an astronaut from Russia, was the first woman in space.

In the following sentences, cross out any letter that should be capitalized. Write the capital letter above it. The first sentence has been done for you.

1. Ellen *O*choa was the first female astronaut who was a *H*ispanic *A*merican.

2. Her grandparents moved from mexico to the united states to raise their family.

3. She was born in los angeles, california.

4. She went to college at stanford university.

5. She was trained at the johnson space center in houston, texas.

6. Her first flight was on april 8, 1993, aboard a space shuttle named *discovery*.

7. Her fellow astronauts on that mission were kenneth d. cameron, kenneth d. cockrell, c. michael foale, and stephen s. oswald.

8. dr. Ochoa has completed several missions, including a trip in April 2002 on the shuttle *atlantis*.

Capital Letters 3

Capitalize the titles of books, movies, poems, magazines, and CD's. In a title, always capitalize the first word and the last word, as well as all the important middle words.

Examples

"The Spelling Test" (poem)

Into the West (movie)

Words like *a*, *the*, *of*, and *and* don't need to be capitalized when they are in the middle of a title.

> **Directions** 〉 In the following titles, cross out each lowercase letter that should be capitalized. Write the capital letter above it. The first one has been done for you.

1.   I   T   L   P   P
    Is there life on a plastic planet? (book)

2. science weekly (magazine)

3. every day is a new day (CD)

4. cat fancy (magazine)

5. jungle book (movie)

6. "mama is a sunrise" (poem)

7. nothing's fair in fifth grade (book)

8. world book encyclopedia (CD)

9. the princess bride (movie)

10. "life doesn't frighten me" (poem)

In the following sentences, cross out any letter that should be capitalized. Write the capital letter above it. The first sentence has been done for you.

1. Even though they are old movies, ~~a~~Aladdin and ~~t~~Toy ~~s~~Story are two of the best.

2. My uncle has all the old *star wars* movies on DVD.

3. Two books I read recently were *wringer* and *joey pigza loses control*.

4. When I am at my grandma's house, I read her old *reader's digest* and *national geographic* magazines.

5. At my dentist's office, I flip through copies of *field and stream*.

6. I have copied "hold fast to dreams," a poem by Langston Hughes, into my notebook.

7. My dad's favorite CD is *come away with me* by Norah Jones.

8. For my birthday, I got a book called *a single shard*. It's about a homeless boy who lives under a bridge in Korea.

NEXT STEP

Write the names of your favorite book, magazine, movie, and CD. Be sure to capitalize the first word, last word, and all other important words in the title.

....

....

....

Capital Letters 4

Capitalize the names of geographic areas, historic events, and documents.

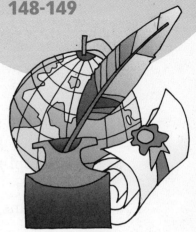

Examples

New England   Mayflower Compact

Great Lakes   Gettysburg Address

Lewis and Clark Expedition   Louisiana Purchase

Directions ⟫ **In the following sentences, cross out any letter that should be capitalized. Write the capital letter above it. The first sentence has been done for you.**

1. The Fourth of July is a celebration of the signing of the ~~d~~D̲eclaration of ~~i~~I̲ndependence.

2. On July 8, 1776, it was published in philadelphia, pennsylvania.

3. Americans no longer wanted to be ruled by King George III of great britain.

4. The boston tea party was a protest of paying taxes to the English.

5. The united states became an independent country.

6. Riders on horseback rode up and down the coast of the atlantic ocean with the exciting news.

7. They carried copies of the document to rhode island, delaware, georgia, and the other colonies.

8. The revolutionary war gave the colonists freedom from their European rulers.

In the following paragraph, cross out any letter that should be capitalized. Write the capital letter above it. The first sentence has been done for you.

1   In the old days, people floated rafts filled with cargo down the

2   ~~m~~ississippi ~~r~~iver. With skill and luck, a raft could float all the way to
     M   *R*

3   new orleans, louisiana. Going upstream was very hard until steam-

4   powered boats came along. In August of 1807, Robert Fulton's

5   steamboat went upstream from new york to albany (150 miles in 32

6   hours). People lined the banks of the hudson river and cheered as the

7   boat went by. Fulton helped the navy in the war of 1812. He lived in

8   a time called the industrial revolution. Think of it as the time when

9   machines started to change america, europe, and the world.

Imagine yourself on a steamboat heading up a river. Write a sentence about it, naming the river you're on.

....

....

....

....

Capital Letters Review

This activity reviews capitalization.

> **Directions** » Add capital letters wherever they are needed by crossing out the lowercase letter and writing the capital above it.

1. alaska is the largest of the 50 states.

2. it is twice the size of texas.

3. to get to alaska by car, you drive across canada for 500 miles.

4. did you know that Alaska's coast is only 50 miles from asia?

5. mount McKinley, the highest mountain in north america, is in Alaska.

6. In 1867, the united states government bought Alaska from russia for about two cents an acre.

7. one-third of Alaska lies within the arctic circle.

8. many native americans live there, including eskimo, or inuit.

9. alaska has a famous 1,200-mile dogsled race called the iditarod.

10. author gary paulsen wrote about the race in a book called *woodsong*.

11. paulsen said, "the dogs are the best thing about racing."

1. on august 21, 1959, Hawaii became our 50th state.

2. hawaii is the newest state in the united states.

3. it had been a u.s. territory since 1900.

4. it's the only state not on the mainland of north america.

5. hawaii is a chain of 132 islands in the pacific ocean.

6. british captain james cook reached Hawaii in 1778.

7. hawaii's last native ruler was queen liliuokalani.

8. on december 7, 1941, the japanese bombed pearl harbor in hawaii.

9. that brought the united states into world war II.

10. one place people like to visit is hawaii volcanoes national park.

11. others tour iolani palace in honolulu, the capital.

12. hawaiians are proud of their mix of polynesian, chinese, japanese, european, and african cultures.

Which state would you rather visit, Alaska or Hawaii? Give one or two reasons. (If you already live in one of these two states, explain what you like about your state.)

....

....

....

Plurals 1

Form most **plurals** by adding *s*. If the word ends in *sh, ch, x, s,* or *z,* add *es* to the singular to form the plural. Some nouns that end in *o* also form the plural by adding *es*.

Examples

fleas   rodeos   foxes   buses   heroes

> **Directions** >> On each line, write the plural of the word in parentheses. The first one has been done for you.

1. My twin _____*sisters*_____ *(sister)* had a graduation picnic.

2. We fastened balloons to both _____ *(porch)*.

3. We lit citronella _____ *(candle)* to keep the bugs away.

4. We tuned two _____ *(radio)* to the same station.

5. Dad started cooking _____ *(hamburger)* on the grill.

6. We had made three heaping _____ *(salad)*.

7. All our _____ *(neighbor)* came to the party.

8. Mrs. Schultz brought egg-salad _____ *(sandwich)*.

9. Slim Ott brought watermelons in two huge _____ *(box)*.

10. As we began to eat, _____ *(flash)* of lightning streaked through the sky.

11. We made several _____ *(dash)* to move the food inside.

Plurals 2

If a noun ends in a consonant before a *y*, drop the *y* and add *ies* to form the plural. If the noun has a vowel before the *y*, just add *s*.

Examples

pony—ponies   **way**—ways

Directions ▶ **On each line, write the plural of the word in parentheses. The first one has been done for you.**

1. We told _____*stories*_____ (*story*) around the campfire.

2. The _____ (*key*) to the house are in the flowerpot.

3. Grandma makes her own _____ (*jelly*) and jams.

4. We loaded our backpacks onto the _____ (*donkey*).

5. _____ (*Army*) of ants attacked the leftovers.

6. _____ (*Fairy*) awakened the princess.

7. Mexico and Spain are Spanish-speaking _____ (*country*).

8. Mexico City and Madrid are their capital _____ (*city*).

9. The _____ (*alley*) in our neighborhood are not paved.

Plurals 3

Nouns that end in *f* or *fe* have their plurals formed in two ways. If you can hear the final *f* in the plural word, just add *s* to the singular noun. If the final *f* has the sound of a *v*, change the *f* to *v* and add *es*.

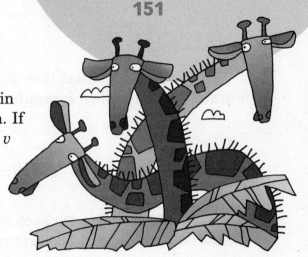

Examples

giraffe—giraffes   **knife—knives**

> **Directions** On each line, write the plural of the word in parentheses. The first one has been done for you.

1. The money was stored in many ____*safes*____ (*safe*).

2. It is said that a cat has nine _____ (*life*).

3. _____ (*Thief*) broke into the music store.

4. They stole three _____ (*fife*) and two drums.

5. Below the _____ (*cliff*), the ocean roared.

6. Red maple _____ (*leaf*) covered the ground.

7. I respect your _____ (*belief*).

8. _____ (*Wolf*) howled in the timberland.

9. The _____ (*shelf*) were packed with trinkets.

10. He repairs _____ (*roof*) for a living.

11. Two _____ (*half*) make a whole.

Plurals 4

There are some nouns that do not follow the rules for plurals. They are called **irregular plurals**. Here are some examples.

Examples

child—children   **goose**—geese   **man**—men

Directions ⟩ On each line, write the plural of the noun in parentheses. The first one has been done for you.

1. There are three ____*feet*____ *(foot)* in a yard.

2. Jana had to get some of her _____ *(tooth)* pulled when she was 10.

3. The _____ *(woman)* organized a canoe trip.

4. Since we got a cat, we have no more _____ *(mouse)*.

5. The _____ *(man)* held their annual pancake breakfast.

6. He rolled the _____ *(die)* to see how many spaces to move on the game board.

7. The _____ *(child)* asked for beanbag chairs in the library.

8. In the fall, the _____ *(goose)* fly to Canada.

9. There were no _____ *(person)* in the parking lot.

10. Three _____ *(woman)* work with my mom.

Abbreviations

Abbreviations are shortened forms of words. Directions, titles, time, and measurements are often given as abbreviations.

Examples

St. (Street)   Mr. (Mister)
p.m. (after noon)   lb. (pound)

> **Directions** >> On the line before each abbreviation on the left, write the letter of the word that matches it. The first one has been done for you.

___*c*___ **1.** N.   **a.** Highway

_____ **2.** St.   **b.** Drive (or Doctor)

_____ **3.** Ave.   **c.** North

_____ **4.** Rd.   **d.** Road

_____ **5.** Rm.   **e.** Avenue

_____ **6.** Hwy.   **f.** Room

_____ **7.** Dr.   **g.** Street

_____ **8.** lb.   **h.** before noon

_____ **9.** Ms.   **i.** ounce

_____ **10.** a.m.   **j.** courtesy title for a woman

_____ **11.** oz.   **k.** pound

_____ **12.** p.m.   **l.** after noon

Directions Write the full word for each abbreviation underlined below. The first one has been done for you.

1   Ralph placed his lunch order at 1:00 p.m. He ordered a
     pound
2   sandwich, a lb. of French fries, and a 64-oz. drink. He asked for his

3   order to be delivered to 1215 Hull Ave.

4   The clerk asked, "What are the cross streets at that address,

5   Mr. Reed?"

6   Ralph told him that they were Asbury St. and Hull Ave., east of

7   Hwy. 10.

8   Then the clerk asked, "Is that near Barry Rd. N. or Quigley

9   Ave.?"

10   Ralph replied, "It's just past Dr. Unger's office on Hull."

11   "Okay, we'll be there soon," said the clerk.

Write directions from your favorite take-out restaurant to your home. Use abbreviations.

....

....

....

Mechanics Review

This activity reviews capitalization, plurals, and abbreviations.

Directions ⟩ **On each line, write the plural or the abbreviation of the words in parentheses.**

1. The _____ (plural of *lady*) were drinking iced tea in the garden.

2. Geraldo hobbled to the house on his _____ (plural of *crutch*).

3. _____ (abbreviation of *doctor*) Luis Santos has opened a new

   eye clinic.

4. It is at the corner of Elm _____ (abbreviation for *Street*) and

   Maple _____ (abbreviation for *Avenue*).

5. "The _____ (plural of *Elf*) and the Shoemaker" is one of

   Grimm's fairy tales.

6. Mom asked me to buy a 5-_____ (abbreviation for *pound*) bag of

   sugar and a 15-_____ (abbreviation for *ounce*) can of tomatoes.

7. The _____ (plural of *baby*) chased the dog around the room.

8. A puppy ripped the sock with its sharp _____ (plural of *tooth*).

9. We got three _____ (plural of *fax*) from my aunt.

10. School starts at 8:00 _____ (abbreviation for *before noon*) and

    ends at 2:30 _____ (abbreviation for *after noon*).

11. Fill all the _____ (plural of *glass*) with ice water.

12. The _____ (plural of *cuff*) on his jacket were tattered and worn.

> **Directions** ▶ If an underlined word is spelled incorrectly, cross it out and write the correct spelling above it. If the underlined word is correct, write "C" above it.

1   In the <u>days</u> before TV, radio was the most popular storyteller in

2   the United States. Families gathered around their big <u>radioes</u> and

3   listened to their favorite <u>shows</u> together. Early radio had some very

4   scary <u>mysterys</u>. Each program had realistic sound <u>effects</u> and a

5   narrator with a creepy voice. The <u>sounds</u> and <u>voices</u> could make your

6   <u>tooths</u> chatter. A good narrator could make you "see" <u>thiefs</u> in dark

7   alleys. A good sound-effects person made <u>leafs</u> rustle, <u>doors</u> creak,

8   <u>wolfs</u> howl, and thunder roll.

9   <u>People</u> cheered for their <u>heros</u> and hoped the bad <u>guys</u> would

10   get caught—which they always did. By the early 1950s, people's <u>lifes</u>

11   changed. TV took over the storytelling business.

Using the Right Word 1

Here are some words that are easily confused. If you remember a few rules, you will be able to use them correctly.

a, an

Use *a* before words that begin with a consonant sound.
My aunt plays a guitar. (consonant sound)

Use *an* before words that begin with any vowel sound except long *u*.
My uncle plays an accordion. (vowel sound)

My cousin plays a ukulele. (long *u* vowel sound)

it's, its

It's so much fun when the band plays its music!
("It's" is the contraction for "it is"; "its" shows possession.)

> **Directions** ⟩ **Write the correct word in each blank. The first one has been done for you.**

1. My aunt and uncle play in ___*a*___ (*a, an*) bluegrass band.

2. My harmonica has _____ (*its, it's*) own carrying case.

3. _____ (*Its, It's*) the only instrument I can play.

4. The band practices for _____ (*a, an*) hour or two each week.

5. They invite me to play _____ (*a, an*) tune or two with them.

6. Playing with good musicians is _____ (*a, an*) honor.

7. Someday I want to play _____ (*a, an*) banjo.

8. I understand that _____ (*its, it's*) very difficult to learn how to

   play, but _____ (*its, it's*) mellow bluegrass sound is worth it.

Using the Right Word 2

Learning the meaning of words can help you use them correctly.

can, may

Can you swim? (Are you able to swim?)

May I go swimming? (You are asking permission.)

threw, through

Threw and *through* are pronounced the same but mean very different things.
I **threw** the beanbag. ("Threw" is an action verb.)
It fell **through** the hole. ("Through" is a preposition.)

> **Directions** >> **Write the correct word in each blank. The first one has been done for you.**

1. I ran _through_ *(threw, through)* the front door.

2. I _____ *(threw, through)* my tag and swim shorts on the counter.

3. "_____ *(Can, May)* I have a locker?" I asked.

4. "You _____ *(can, may)* have one soon," the attendant said.

5. "I _____ *(can, may)* wait," I said.

6. I leafed _____ *(threw, through)* a magazine.

7. "You _____ *(can, may)* go in now," the attendant said.

8. "I _____ *(can, may)* hardly wait to dive in," I said.

9. "Here," he said as he _____ *(threw, through)* me my swim shorts.

Using the Right Word 3

Here are two more sets of words that are often confused: *quiet, quit, quite* and *than, then*. Use the "Proofreader's Guide" to help you know when to use each.

Examples

Though Tim is quiet, he is quite smart. If he has problems, he does not quit.

Tim said, "I am smarter than you are." Then he walked right into the glass door.

> **Directions** Write the correct word in each blank. The first one has been done for you.

1   Adam did not have a ___*quiet*___ *(quiet, quit, quite)* day at school.

2   First, his thermos broke, and he had _____ *(quiet, quit, quite)* a

3   mess in his lunchbox. The bus was later _____ *(than, then)*

4   yesterday, and _____ *(than, then)* the person selling milk had only

5   whole milk.

6   "I like skim milk more _____ *(than, then)* whole milk," Adam

7   said. _____ *(Than, Then)* the boy before Adam bought his hot

8   lunch with 150 pennies. Adam waited while the attendant counted all

9   those pennies, though he was in _____ *(quiet, quit, quite)* a hurry.

10   Adam wanted to _____ *(quiet, quit, quite)* school for the day.

11   He wanted to go home for some peace and _____ *(quiet, quit, quite)*.

Using the Right Word 4

Simple clues can help you with confusing words.

knew, new

I **knew** you got a special present. ("Knew" is the past tense of "know.")

Can I see your **new** puppy? ("New" is the opposite of "old.")

already, all ready

I am **already** late. ("Already" is an adverb telling when.)

Are you **all ready**? ("All ready" means "completely ready.")

Directions ➤ Write the correct word in each blank. The first one has been done for you.

1. We were __all ready__ (already, all ready) to play ball.

2. I _____ (knew, new) I would like my sister's _____ (knew, new) boyfriend.

3. Jonah waxed his car so it would look like _____ (knew, new).

4. One hot day, I _____ (knew, new) I wanted to swim in the _____ (knew, new) pool.

5. I wish I _____ (knew, new) more about the ocean.

6. Are you _____ (already, all ready) for the big surprise?

7. Some _____ (knew, new) cars run on electricity.

8. We were _____ (already, all ready) out the door before she called.

9. Is everything _____ (already, all ready) for the birthday party?

10. Grandpa didn't like the _____ (knew, new) shopping center.

Using the Right Word Review

This activity reviews using the easily confused words that you have studied.

Directions ⟫ If an underlined word is incorrect, cross it out and write the correct word above it. If the underlined word is correct, write "C" above it.

1 Is there a harder sporting event <u>then</u> the Tour de France? <u>It's</u>

2 <u>a</u> amazing bicycle race that takes place in France each July. This race

3 is <u>quit</u> a test of strength and skill. You <u>may</u> enter the Tour de France

4 only if you are <u>all ready</u> one of the top cyclists in the world.

5 Cyclists take their bikes, <u>new</u> bike parts (for breakdowns), and

6 support teams with them. <u>Than</u> they bike 2,400 miles <u>through</u>

7 France. Biking <u>through</u> flat land and <u>quiet</u> villages would be fun. (<u>Its</u>

8 at the first towering mountain that I'd want to <u>quit</u>!) The race

9 participants must ride <u>threw</u> sunshine and rain for three weeks until

10 they complete the race at <u>it's</u> finish line in Paris.

If an underlined word is incorrect, cross it out and write the correct word above it. If the underlined word is correct, write "C" above it.

1   From an early age, Lance Armstrong wanted to be <u>a</u>

2   outstanding athlete. He learned about discipline and training <u>threw</u>

3   triathlons in which he ran, biked, and swam. A triathlon is <u>quite</u> an

4   exhausting event. <u>Its</u> a definite challenge for most people. Lance soon

5   discovered that he enjoyed biking more <u>then</u> he enjoyed running and

6   swimming.

7   In 1996, he had to <u>quite</u> bike racing. He had a fast-growing

8   cancer, and he <u>knew</u> he had to stop <u>its</u> spread. He <u>through</u> himself

9   into treatment and getting well. He did it in the same way he had

10   thrown himself into training and winning races.

11   In 1999, he was <u>already</u> for the big race, the Tour de France.

12   <u>Through</u> hard work and determination, he won that race and <u>than</u>

13   went on to win many more. He inspired cancer patients all over the

14   world who said, "If Lance Armstrong <u>can</u> do something so amazing

15   with his life, perhaps my case isn't hopeless either."

Sentence Activities

The activities in this section cover three important writing areas: (1) the basic parts, types, and kinds of sentences; (2) common sentence errors; and (3) methods for writing smooth-reading sentences. All of the activities include helpful "Proofreader's Guide" references. Most activities also include a **Next Step** that offers follow-up practice for certain skills.

Simple Subjects

Every sentence has a subject. A **simple subject** is the subject all alone without any of the other words that describe it.

Examples

Mr. Williamson, a wonderful neighbor, helped me rake the yard.

The neon-yellow bike raced down the street.

> **Directions** > Underline the simple subject in each sentence. The first one has been done for you.

1. Alicia, my best friend since kindergarten, is moving away.

2. The pilgrims at Plymouth Rock faced many problems.

3. The rainbow's bright colors melted into the pale blue sky.

4. The Hobbit was a curious little fellow.

5. The constellations of stars stay the same in the sky.

6. Lucas went to Chicago with his school's stamp club.

> **Directions** > Write two sentences that each have one subject. Underline the simple subject in each sentence.

1. ....

   ....

2. ....

   ....

Compound Subjects

Some sentences have compound subjects. A **compound subject** has two or more simple subjects.

Examples

Folktales and fables have interesting characters.

Luis, Ricky, and Kyle read about the fox and the grapes.

> **Directions** Decide if these sentences have simple or compound subjects. On each blank, write "S" for a simple subject or "C" for a compound subject. The first one has been done for you.

_C_ **1.** Benjamin Franklin and Paul Revere were patriots of the American Revolution.

_____ **2.** Tacos and burritos are my favorite things to eat.

_____ **3.** Lizzy has a brown-and-white horse.

_____ **4.** The puzzle was hard to complete.

_____ **5.** Whales and sharks live in the ocean.

_____ **6.** Independence Day is also known as the Fourth of July.

_____ **7.** Mary Pickersgill and her daughter were flag makers.

_____ **8.** Sacagawea traveled with Lewis and Clark.

_____ **9.** Travis, Antwon, and Owen played basketball all morning.

_____ **10.** The beautiful stones and fossils were buried in dirt.

Read the 10 sentences above. Underline the simple subjects.

Simple Predicates (Verbs)

Every sentence has a predicate, or verb. A predicate tells what the subject is doing, or it tells something about the subject. A **simple predicate** is the verb all alone without any of the words that describe it.

Examples

Paul Revere's horse **galloped** on cobblestone streets.

Seawater **tastes** salty.

Directions ▶ Complete these sentences by writing a verb on each blank. The first one has been done for you.

1. The old school _____*looks*_____ like an old castle.

2. The colonists _____ a variety of vegetables.

3. My best friend and I _____ on Saturdays.

4. Squirrels _____ nuts in the park by my house.

5. The stars _____ in the summer sky.

6. Alexander Graham Bell _____ the telephone.

7. The basketball player _____ the ball toward the basket.

8. Charlie _____ through the muddy field.

9. Kayla and Rita _____ to school on a city bus.

10. The taxi _____ over the railroad tracks.

Compound Predicates

Some sentences have compound predicates. A **compound predicate** is two or more simple predicates (verbs) in a sentence.

Examples

Rusty jumped in the puddle and raced through the weeds.

Tanya washed, combed, and brushed the dog's tangled fur.

> **Directions** Decide whether these sentences have simple or compound predicates. On each blank, write "S" for a simple predicate or "C" for a compound predicate. The first one has been done for you.

_S_ 1. The colonists remained strong and brave.

_____ 2. Betsy Ross sewed an American flag.

_____ 3. Lightning zigzagged through the sky and struck the tree.

_____ 4. Cool water ripples over the stones in the riverbed.

_____ 5. The teachers sang, danced, and told jokes in the variety show.

_____ 6. A rattlesnake slithered through the tall grass.

_____ 7. Laura Ingalls traveled in a covered wagon and lived on a prairie.

_____ 8. My pal, Benny, always chews gum.

_____ 9. May Lee and her sister, Sue, live above a restaurant.

_____ 10. Dad and I went to the barber and got haircuts.

Read the 10 sentences above. Circle each simple predicate.

Clauses 1

A **clause** is a group of words in a sentence. A clause always has a subject and a verb. An **independent clause** is a complete thought that can stand alone as a sentence.

Examples

The tree grew tall.

The leaves fell from the top branches.

 **Directions** ▶ Underline the subject and circle the verb in each of these independent clauses. The first one has been done for you.

1. The <u>starship</u> (landed) on the green planet.

2. Aliens waited quietly in a nearby cave.

3. They watched the strange-looking astronauts.

4. Suddenly, the astronauts saw someone.

5. Maybe life exists on this strange, green planet.

Directions ▶ Write three independent clauses about space travel. Underline the subjects and circle the verbs.

1. ....

....

2. ....

....

3. ....

....

Clauses 2

A **dependent clause** cannot stand alone as a sentence, even though it has both a subject and a verb. Dependent clauses begin with either a subordinating conjunction or a relative pronoun.

Examples

after they lost the game
(This dependent clause begins with the subordinating conjunction "after.")

who hit the final run
(This dependent clause begins with the relative pronoun "who.")

Directions ▶ Decide if these are independent or dependent clauses. On each blank, write "I" for an independent clause or "D" for a dependent clause. The first one has been done for you.

__D__ 1. When I got up this morning

_____ 2. I love Independence Day

_____ 3. Fireworks rained from the sky

_____ 4. After the band marched by

_____ 5. Uncle Sam walked atop tall, striped stilts

Directions ▶ Create complete sentences by adding an independent clause after each dependent clause below. Notice that the clauses are separated by a comma.

1. When we went outside, ...

....

2. Since it was dark, ...

....

Simple and Compound Sentences

A **simple sentence** has one main idea.

The truck driver dumped a load of dirt.

A **compound sentence** is two simple sentences joined by a comma and a connecting word (*and, but, so, or*).

The truck driver dumped a load of dirt, **but** he was at the wrong address.

> **Directions** On the line before each sentence, write "S" for simple or "C" for compound. The first one has been done for you.

_S___ **1.** *Anne of Green Gables* is my favorite book.

_____ **2.** The main character is Anne Shirley, and she is an orphan.

_____ **3.** Anne lives with Matthew and Marilla Cuthbert.

_____ **4.** Anne's closest friend is Diana Barry.

_____ **5.** Diana goes to Anne's for a snack, and she gets very sick.

_____ **6.** Anne gets blamed for making Diana sick, but it is not her fault.

_____ **7.** Diana's mother is angry with Anne, so Anne feels sad.

_____ **8.** Then Diana's little sister gets sick, and Anne saves her life.

_____ **9.** After that, Diana's mother forgives Anne.

_____ **10.** The girls are best friends forever and ever.

Write three simple sentences and three compound sentences that answer the following questions.

1. Simple Sentence 1: What is the name of your favorite book?

....

2. Simple Sentence 2: Who is the main character in the story?

....

3. Simple Sentence 3: Where does the story take place?

....

4. Compound Sentence 1: What problem does the main character face?

....

....

5. Compound Sentence 2: What are two important events in the story?

....

....

6. Compound Sentence 3: What are two reasons for liking this book?

....

....

Trade papers with a classmate. Check to make sure that the sentences are correct.

Complex Sentences

A **complex sentence** has one independent clause and one or more dependent clauses. A dependent clause can come at the beginning or at the end of a sentence. Remember, dependent clauses begin with a subordinating conjunction or a relative pronoun.

Examples

I walk to school with Maria, who lives next door.
(The dependent clause at the end of the sentence begins with the relative pronoun "who.")

When Towanda is near the flowers, she sneezes.
(The dependent clause at the beginning of the sentence begins with the subordinating conjunction "when.")

Directions ▶ Write "complex" on the line before each complex sentence. The first one has been done for you.

complex **1.** Mr. Tony is the pet shop owner who taught me about goldfish.

_____ **2.** He sells goldfish, and he knows a lot about them.

_____ **3.** Goldfish can live in bowls, or they can live in ponds.

_____ **4.** Goldfish are good pets because they are easy to care for.

_____ **5.** Feed goldfish every day, but don't feed them too much.

_____ **6.** Since goldfish can get sick in dirty water, keep the water clean.

1. Ben said his brother could go along <u>if he was quiet</u>.

2. The walk was led by Mr. Lee, who was my third-grade teacher.

3. Although he looked fine, Elhadji said he felt sick.

4. We walked through the maze until we got to the end.

5. I like fizzy soda because it makes my nose tickle.

6. Since it was storming outside, students stayed in from recess.

7. The old shopkeeper put on his glasses in order that he could see.

8. Sacagawea was a Shoshoni Indian who guided Lewis and Clark.

9. Washington, D.C., is important because it is the nation's capital.

10. After the tornado went through, there were few trees left.

Write two dependent clauses. Trade papers with a classmate and complete each other's sentences by adding an independent clause to each.

Prepositional Phrases

Prepositions are words that show position or direction and introduce a prepositional phrase. A **prepositional phrase** has a preposition and the object of the preposition. Sometimes a prepositional phrase has describing words, too.

Examples

The rabbit dug underneath the white picket fence.
He ate everything in our vegetable garden.

> **Directions** ▶▶ Underline the prepositional phrases in the sentences below. The first one has been done for you.

1. A strange creature skittered down the alley.

2. Cal saw it run under some boxes.

3. He wondered if he should tell any of his friends.

4. Others had heard about it at school that day.

5. A small creature was seen in Milward's Park.

6. Could that be what Cal saw run across the street?

7. The sheriff said, "Don't go near it."

8. Perhaps this creature escaped from a local pet store or zoo.

Read the sentences on the previous page. Then write two or three sentences to finish the story. Include and underline a prepositional phrase in each sentence.

....

....

....

....

....

....

....

....

....

....

....

Read your story aloud to a friend. Make sure that each sentence includes at least one prepositional phrase.

Declarative Sentences

A **declarative sentence** is a statement that tells something about a person, a place, a thing, or an idea. A declarative sentence ends with a period.

Examples

Cherry trees have pretty blossoms in the spring.
Each blossom can turn into a cherry.
I like sweet cherries better than sour ones.

Directions	Write five declarative sentences about something that interests you. You might want to tell about something that you learned in school or about a hobby, a place, or a sport that you like. (Remember to end each sentence with a period.)

1. ....

....

2. ....

....

3. ....

....

4. ....

....

5. ....

....

Imperative Sentences

An **imperative sentence** gives a command or makes a request. An imperative sentence also ends with a period.

Examples

Climb the cherry tree.
Pick some cherries.
Please put them in the bucket.

Directions >> Write imperative sentences that tell how to get from your house to your school, a friend's house, or a grocery store. Remember to end each sentence with a period.

....

....

....

....

....

....

....

....

Write simple directions for a partner to follow. They can be silly if you want them to be. If you write clear imperative sentences, your partner will have no problem following your directions.

Interrogative Sentences

An **interrogative sentence** asks a question, so it ends with a question mark.

Examples
    Did you know that the cherry blossom is Japan's national flower?
    What kinds of animals like to eat cherries?
    Do you like chocolate-covered cherries?

Directions ▶ Write five interrogative sentences. Ask questions about something that really interests you. (Remember to end each sentence with a question mark.)

1. Who ....

....

2. What ....

....

3. When ....

....

4. Where ....

....

5. Why ....

....

Exclamatory Sentences

An **exclamatory sentence** shows strong emotion or surprise. An exclamatory sentence ends with an exclamation point.

Examples

A crow stole my cherries!
I got stung by a bee!

Directions ▶ Pretend that you are hiking and discover some strange-looking things. Write five exclamatory sentences to tell about them. (Remember to use exclamation points.)

1. ....

2. ....

3. ....

4. ....

5. ....

NEXT STEP

Remember the four kinds of sentences—declarative, imperative, interrogative, and exclamatory. Write one sentence of each kind.

....

....

....

Sentence Fragments 1

A **sentence fragment** does not express a complete idea. It is missing a subject, a verb, or sometimes a subject and a verb.

Examples

Hit the ball through the window.
(The subject is missing in this fragment.)

My friends Alex and Danny.
(The verb is missing in this fragment.)

Not much fun.
(The subject and the verb are missing in this fragment.)

Directions 〉〉 Decide if these are sentences or fragments. On each blank, write "S" for a sentence or "F" for a fragment. The first one has been done for you.

____*S*____ **1.** Sal sings in the choir.

_____ **2.** Meets after school on Wednesdays.

_____ **3.** Sal's friend in the choir, too.

_____ **4.** They learn songs from around the world.

_____ **5.** To sing in other languages.

_____ **6.** About people in other countries.

_____ **7.** Sal sang with a choir from Africa.

_____ **8.** Is pen pals with one of the African choir members.

_____ **9.** I would like to join the choir, too.

_____ **10.** Fun to learn new songs.

Look back at the fragments on the previous page. Decide if the fragment is missing a subject, a verb, or both. On the lines below, rewrite each fragment as a complete sentence.

1. ....

....

2. ....

....

3. ....

....

4. ....

....

5. ....

....

6. ....

....

Sentence Fragments 2

On these pages, you will practice fixing
sentence fragments. You have already learned
that a fragment is missing a subject, a verb, or
sometimes a subject and a verb.

Directions ▶▶ On each blank, write "S" for a missing subject, "V" for a
missing verb, or "S+V" for a missing subject and verb.
Then fix the fragment; write a complete sentence on the
lines. The first one has been done for you.

_**S**_ **1.** Is Lightning Awareness Week

This week is Lightning Awareness Week.

_____ **2.** All about lightning

....

....

_____ **3.** Can be very dangerous

....

....

_____ **4.** Very quickly

....

....

_____ **5.** Are killed every year by lightning

....

....

_____ **6.** Means that a storm is near

....

....

_____ **7.** See lightning first

....

....

_____ **8.** Then thunder

....

....

_____ **9.** Inside the best place to be

....

....

_____ **10.** Can hurt or kill you

....

....

Trade papers with a partner. Did you fix the sentences the same way?

Run-On Sentences 1

A **run-on sentence** happens when two or
more sentences run together. One way to fix this
error is to split the sentence into two complete
sentences.

Example

Run-On Sentence: We went to Atlanta it is Georgia's capital city.
Corrected Sentence: We went to Atlanta. It is Georgia's capital city.

> **Directions** ▶ Fix these run-on sentences by changing them into two
> complete sentences. The first one has been done for you.

1. Washington, D.C., has lots to see I love the monuments.

Washington, D.C., has lots to see. I love the monuments.

2. The Washington Monument is 555 feet tall I went to the top of it.

....

....

3. The Lincoln Memorial has a huge statue of President Lincoln he is
sitting in a chair.

....

....

....

4. You should visit these monuments they are amazing and educational.

....

....

Run-On Sentences 2

Another way to fix a **run-on sentence** is to make it
a compound sentence. You can do that by adding a comma and
a connecting word (*and, but, or, so, yet*).

Example

Run-On Sentence:

Our class went to the nation's capital we saw many museums.

Corrected Sentence:

Our class went to the nation's capital**,** **and** we saw many museums.

> **Directions** In the following paragraph, look for run-on sentences. Fix them by inserting a comma and a connecting word ("and," "but," "or," "yet"). The first one has been done for you.

1   The National Air and Space Museum is in Washington, D.C.

2   It opened in 1976 on America's 200th birthday**,** *and* millions of people

3   have visited it. There are many planes on display the *Spirit of*

4   *St. Louis* is the most famous plane on exhibit. Charles

5   Lindbergh flew it alone across the Atlantic Ocean. The flight

6   was long and dangerous he flew from New York to Paris. People

7   nicknamed him Lucky Lindy. At the National Air and Space

8   Museum, you can see rockets, planes, and space capsules you

9   can choose to sit back and watch movies about space.

Trade papers with a partner. Did you correct sentences in the same way?

Rambling Sentences

A **rambling sentence** happens when too many short sentences are connected with the word *and*.

Example

Rambling Sentence: We went to the grocery store and bought meat, eggs, and butter, and then we went to the post office and got stamps, and after that, we went to Hamburger Henry's for lunch.

Corrected Sentences: We went to the grocery store and bought meat, eggs, and butter. Then we went to the post office and got stamps. After that, we went to Hamburger Henry's for lunch.

 **Directions** Fix the following rambling sentence. Rewrite it below, dividing it into as many sentences as you think are needed.

Harriet Tubman's slave name was Aramita Ross and when she was eleven, she took her mother's name, Harriet, and she spent most of her childhood working as a slave, and sometimes she worked on nearby plantations, and Harriet was beaten and mistreated, and one day she decided to run away, and she found her way to freedom and then she helped other slaves to become free.

....

....

....

....

....

....

....

Double Negatives

Do not use two or more negative words, like *never* and *no* or *not* and *no*, in the same sentence.

Example

Double Negative: I **didn't** make **no** mistakes on my spelling test.
Corrected Sentences: I **didn't** make **any** mistakes on my spelling test.
I made **no** mistakes on my spelling test.

> **Directions** ▶ Correct the double negatives in these sentences. Write the revised sentences on the lines. The first one has been done for you.

1. I didn't have no time to do my homework.

I didn't have any time to do my homework.

2. I don't want no more popcorn.

....

3. He can't find none of his favorite CD's.

....

....

4. Regina doesn't have no money to go to a movie.

....

....

5. Tyrone can't go nowhere with us on Sunday.

....

....

Double Subjects

A **double subject** usually happens when you put a pronoun right after the subject.

Examples

Double Subjects:
Jeremy **he** has a new basketball.
Karen and Lisa **they** went to the ball game.

Corrected Sentences:
Jeremy has a new basketball.
Karen and Lisa went to the ball game.

> **Directions** >> Fix the double subjects in the following sentences by crossing out the extra pronoun. The first one has been done for you.

1. Costas and Levon ~~they~~ decided to go to summer camp.

2. Levon he had never been to summer camp.

3. His sister she had been to summer camp twice.

4. She and Costas they had been at the same camp.

5. Levon he felt left out because he didn't know about camping.

6. Costas he said, "Don't worry, Levon."

7. He added, "Your sister and I we will tell you all about it."

8. Costas and Levon's sister they told him what to expect at camp.

9. By the time he went to camp, Levon he wasn't worried at all.

10. Costas and Levon they had a great time hiking, swimming, and

    canoeing at camp.

Fix the the double subjects in the following sentences by crossing out the extra pronoun. If a sentence is correct, write "C" on the line before the sentence. The first one has been done for you.

_____C_____ **1.** The ocean floor is littered with shipwrecks.

_____ **2.** The waters off Florida ~~they~~ hold thousands of shipwrecks.

_____ **3.** The most interesting wrecks ~~they~~ are Spain's treasure ships.

_____ **4.** Spanish ships ~~they~~ were called caravels and galleons.

_____ **5.** A treasure ship carried about 200 sailors.

_____ **6.** The lower deck ~~it~~ had a room filled with gold and silver.

_____ **7.** A guard ~~he~~ watched over the treasures.

_____ **8.** Some Florida museums have treasures taken from these ships.

_____ **9.** Some of the treasures ~~they~~ washed up on the beaches.

_____ **10.** You may keep any gold coins you find on Florida's beaches.

Write a short story about a shipwreck. Make sure your sentences don't have double subjects.

Combining Sentences with Key Words

You can combine sentences by moving a **key word** (usually an adjective or adverb) from one sentence to another.

Example

Short Sentences:
Darrice had a party. It was fun.

Combined Sentence:
Darrice had a fun party.

> **Directions** » Move a key word in order to combine each pair of short sentences into one sentence. Underline the key word you use. The first one has been done for you.

1. Darrice put on a mask. It was a <u>silly</u> mask.

   Darrice put on a silly mask.
   ....

2. She wore the mask to Lisa's party. She wore it yesterday.

   ....

3. Everyone laughed. They laughed loudly.

   ....

4. Darrice is my friend. She is hilarious.

   ....

5. I borrowed Darrice's mask. I borrowed it Thursday.

   ....

Choose a sentence from Box A. Choose another sentence from Box B. Use a key word to combine the two sentences. Write the new sentences on the lines.

A

My dad snores.
I read a story.
I am going to the ball game.
I found a kitten.
Tom lost his key.

B

The kitten was tiny.
He lost it yesterday.
I am going later.
He snores loudly.
It was a true story.

1. ....

....

2. ....

....

3. ....

....

4. ....

....

5. ....

....

Read your sentences aloud to a classmate.

Combining Sentences with a Series of Words or Phrases

You can combine short sentences by using a **series of words or phrases**. The series words are separated by commas.

Example

Short Sentences: We like to play basketball at Kevin's house.
Sometimes we play at the recreation center.
We also play at the park.

Combined Sentence: We like to play basketball at Kevin's house, at the recreation center, and at the park.

> **Directions** >> Use a series of words or phrases to combine each set of short sentences. The first one has been done for you.

1. Paul put chocolate syrup on his ice cream. He also put whipped cream on it. He put a cherry on it, too.

Paul put chocolate syrup, whipped cream, and a cherry on his ice cream.

2. It was hot outside. It was dark. It was steamy.

3. At school we study history. We study math. We study science.

4. The farmer had cows in the barn. Cows were in the pasture. Others were by the house.

> **Ask a classmate for words to fill in the blanks in these short sentences. Then combine them into one sentence using a series of words or phrases.**

1. The cake was _____. It was _____.

It was _____.

....

2. The new planet had a _____. It also had a _____.

It had a _____, too.

....

....

3. Apes are _____. They are _____.

They are _____, too.

....

....

4. When I was on vacation, I saw a _____. I saw a

_____. I also saw a big _____.

....

....

5. The skunk _____. It _____.

Then it _____.

....

....

Combining Sentences with Compound Subjects and Verbs

You can combine sentences by moving a subject or verb from one sentence to another. By doing this, you make a **compound subject** or **compound verb**.

Examples

Short Sentences: Sacagawea was a Shoshoni Indian.
Leaping Fish was a Shoshoni Indian, too.

Compound Subject: Sacagawea and Leaping Fish were Shoshoni Indians.

Short Sentences: These friends traveled together. They hunted for buffalo.

Compound Verb: These friends traveled together and hunted for buffalo.

 **Directions** ▶ Combine these sentences by using a compound subject or compound verb. The first one has been done for you.

1. Food came from buffalo. Clothing came from buffalo, too.

   Food and clothing came from buffalo.

2. Buffalo roamed the plains. Buffalo grazed there for food.

   ....

   ....

3. Sacagawea wanted a warm buffalo robe. Leaping Fish wanted one, too.

   ....

   ....

Ask a classmate for words to fill in the blanks in the short sentences. Then combine the short sentences using a compound subject or compound verb.

1. My friend has a _____. I have one, too.

....

2. _____ plays _____.

_____ also plays _____.

....

3. Lions can _____. They also can _____.

....

....

4. Olga found a _____. Kristen also found a _____.

....

....

5. The cat _____. It also _____.

....

....

6. Chris _____. Then he _____.

....

....

Combining Sentences with Coordinating Conjunctions

A **coordinating conjunction** (*and, but, or, so*) can be used to connect two simple sentences. A comma always goes before the conjunction.

Example

Short Sentences: We went to the fair. We had an awesome time.
Combined Sentence: We went to the fair, **and** we had an awesome time.

> **Directions** Combine each pair of short sentences using a comma and a coordinating conjunction. The first one has been done for you.

1. We could go see the animals. We could go to the midway.

We could go see the animals, or we could go to the midway.

2. We decided to see the animals first. We would go to the midway last.

_____

_____

3. I thought the pig barn would be empty. There was a crowd.

_____

_____

4. A mother pig had piglets. Everyone wanted to see them.

_____

_____

Combining Sentences with Subordinating Conjunctions

You can combine sentences by using a **subordinating conjunction** to form a complex sentence. Remember, a complex sentence has a dependent and an independent clause.

Example

Short Sentences: Jenny held the puppy. The vet gave it a shot.

Combined Sentence: Jenny held the puppy while the vet gave it a shot.

> **Directions** » Choose a subordinating conjunction from this list to complete these complex sentences. Use each one only once. The first one has been done for you.

if	because	since	until	before	as long as	so that

1. Ryan used a canoe instead of a motorboat __so that__ no one would hear him go.

2. He would be safe _____ he was very quiet.

3. He had waited _____ darkness fell.

4. He would miss the old house _____ it once held happy memories.

5. _____ he wanted to cross the river before dawn, Ryan paddled hard.

6. He wanted to get to Aunt Marge's house _____ she left for work.

7. Aunt Marge would surely take Ryan in _____ she loved him.

Combining Sentences Review

This activity reviews combining sentences with key words, series of words and phrases, compound verbs, and coordinating conjunctions.

Directions 〉 Combine the following sentences using the skills you practiced. If you need help, look back on the listed pages.

1. "Ryan," a voice whispered, "I'm scared." It was a tiny voice. (*key word*, pages 77-78)

....

....

2. Ryan looked toward the back of the canoe. He saw his little brother Teddy. (*coordinating conjunction*, page 83)

....

....

....

3. Teddy looked scared. He looked sad. He also looked tired. (*series of words*, pages 79-80)

....

....

4. Teddy said, "I watched you pack. I watched you walk to the woods. I watched you get into the canoe." (*series of phrases*, pages 79-80)

....

....

5. "You forgot your backpack. You went back to the house," he said. (*coordinating conjunction*, page 83)

....

....

6. "That's when I ran to the canoe. I hid inside," Teddy admitted. (*compound verb*, pages 81-82)

....

....

7. Ryan stopped paddling. Ryan decided what to do. (*compound verb*, pages 81-82)

....

....

Write the ending to Ryan's story using a variety of sentences.

....

....

....

....

Parts of Speech Activities

The activities in this section review the eight parts of speech. All of the activities include helpful "Proofreader's Guide" references. In addition, the **Next Step** activities offer follow-up practice for certain skills.

Nouns

A **noun** names a person, a place, a thing, or an idea. Here is an example of each type.

Examples

Person	Place	Thing	Idea
girl	store	tractor	freedom
cowboy	kitchen	book	fear
neighbor	street	spider	pride
nurse	desert	carrot	glory

Directions ▸ Underline the nouns in the following sentences. (The number at the end of each sentence tells you how many nouns are in that sentence.) The first one has been done for you.

1. Who takes out the <u>trash</u> at your <u>house</u>? *(2)*

2. In our <u>family</u>, it's my <u>job</u>. *(2)*

3. What happens to all this <u>junk</u>? *(1)*

4. Most of it is dumped into <u>landfills</u>. *(1)*

5. One <u>town</u> had a great <u>idea</u>. *(2)*

6. They made a big <u>hill</u> out of the <u>garbage</u>. *(2)*

7. They covered it with thick <u>plastic</u>. *(1)*

8. Then they added <u>dirt</u> and <u>grass</u>. *(2)*

9. In <u>winter</u>, <u>kids</u> watch for the first good <u>snow</u>. *(3)*

10. They haul out <u>sleds</u>, <u>skis</u>, and even old <u>trays</u>! *(3)*

11. Soon they are sliding down their homegrown "<u>mountain</u>." *(1)*

Underline the nouns in the following story. (The number at the end of each sentence tells you how many nouns to look for in that sentence.) The first sentence has been done for you.

1   Every <u>spring</u> our <u>neighborhood</u> has a cleanup <u>day</u>. *(3)* Men,

2   women, and children walk around picking up trash. *(4)* We fill bags

3   with glass, paper, cans, bottles, and wrappings from fast-food

4   restaurants. *(7)* Then we head for the park. *(1)* Some people must

5   think the park is a dump. *(3)* You would be surprised by the things

6   we find. *(1)* I spotted a rusty bike under the bushes and a doll

7   without a head. *(4)* Once I found a nice watch, but it didn't run. *(1)*

8   We always find a single shoe, never a pair. *(2)* Is someone walking

9   around town with one shoe? *(2)* There are many mysteries when it

10   comes to trash. *(2)*

Think about the best ways to stop litterbugs. Write your ideas in two or three sentences. Underline the nouns.

....

....

....

Common and Proper Nouns

A **common noun** is the general name for a person, a place, a thing, or an idea. A **proper noun** is the specific name of a person, a place, a thing, or an idea. Proper nouns are capitalized.

Examples

Common Nouns	Proper Nouns
explorer	Matthew Henson
ocean	Arctic Ocean

Directions ▶ Underline all the nouns in the following sentences. (The number at the end of each line tells you how many words are nouns.) Write "PN" above the proper nouns. The first sentence has been done for you.

1. Two <u>men</u> reached the <u>North Pole</u> in <u>1909</u>. *(3)*
              PN

2. It was a long, dangerous <u>journey</u>. *(1)*

3. <u>Robert Peary</u>, an <u>explorer</u>, hired <u>Matthew Henson</u>. *(3)*

4. <u>Henson</u>, an <u>African American</u>, quickly became an excellent <u>sailor</u>. *(3)*

5. He could steer a <u>ship</u> by looking at the <u>stars</u>. *(2)*

6. He learned the <u>language</u> of the <u>natives</u> in the <u>Arctic</u>. *(3)*

7. On the <u>trail</u>, <u>Henson</u> usually led. *(2)*

8. Some <u>people</u> think he got to the <u>pole</u> first. *(2)*

9. <u>Peary</u> got most of the <u>credit</u> at the <u>time</u>. *(3)*

10. Later, <u>Henson</u> got the <u>honor</u> he deserved. *(2)*

Write a proper noun to go with each common noun. Then write a common noun to go with each proper noun.

Common Nouns	Proper Nouns
1. pet's name	....
2. lake	....
3. mountain	....
4. magazine	....
5. man	....
6. month	....
7.	Glacier National Park
8.	Monday
9.	Memorial Day
10.	"Star-Spangled Banner"
11.	Chinese
12.	George Washington

NEXT STEP

Write the name of your town, state, country, continent, and planet.

....

....

....

....

Singular and Plural Nouns

A **singular noun** names one person, place, thing, or idea. A **plural noun** names more than one person, place, thing, or idea. Most plural nouns are formed by adding *s* to the singular noun.

Examples

Singular Nouns	Plural Nouns
ZOO bottle	ZOOS bottles

Directions ▶ Change each of the nouns in parentheses to a plural noun. Write the plural noun on the line to complete the sentence. The first one has been done for you.

1. Long ago, people in Greece respected ___reptiles___ (reptile).

2. They believed these creatures had healing __powers__ (power).

3. ___Snakes___ (Snake) shed and regrow their skins each year.

4. Greek __temples__ (temple) kept "sacred" snakes around.

5. Those __customs__ (custom) died out, thank goodness!

6. Some __lizards__ (lizard) seem amazing, too.

7. They can grow new __tails__ (tail) when their old ones break off.

8. Lizards and snakes are not magical __beings__ (being).

9. They help __humans__ (human) and the environment.

10. Without them, there would be lots of __insects__ (insect).

Write the names of six animals that you have seen (or would like to see) at the zoo. Then write the plurals of those nouns.

Singular Nouns   **Plural Nouns**

1. ....

2. ....

3. ....

4. ....

5. ....

6. ....

NEXT STEP

Choose one of the animals on your list. Write three sentences about this creature. (Think about why you are interested in this animal, how it acts, and what it looks like.) Circle all the nouns in your sentences.

....

....

....

....

....

Personal Pronouns

Pronouns are words that are used in place of nouns. A subject pronoun is used as the subject of a sentence (*I, he, she, we, they*). If a pronoun is not the subject, it may be an object pronoun (*me, him, her, us, them*). An object pronoun is used after an action verb or in a prepositional phrase.

Examples

I like adventure stories. ("I" is a subject pronoun.)

Mysteries interest me most. ("Me" is an object pronoun.)

> **Directions** Underline all the pronouns in these sentences. Write "S" above each subject pronoun. Write "O" above each object pronoun. The first one has been done for you.

1. Mrs. Henry assigned us the book *Holes* by Louis Sachar.

2. The book gave me chills and thrills.

3. We all thought Stanley, the main character, was brave and cool.

4. He was accused of stealing and was sent to a reform school.

5. The best thing that happened to him was meeting Zero, another "inmate."

6. They ran off together and had many scary adventures.

7. In one part, lizards were sliding all over them.

8. They survived by eating wild onions!

9. I thought *Holes* was a great book.

Write the correct pronoun in each blank. The first one has been done for you.

1. ___He___ (*He, Him*) pitched the ball.

2. _____ (*She, Her*) smacked it down the middle.

3. The ball came straight back at _____ (*he, him*).

4. It almost knocked _____ (*he, him*) down.

5. _____ (*She, Her*) threw the bat and stumbled.

6. The coach screamed at _____ (*she, her*), "Run!"

7. _____ (*I, Me*) saw the dogs first.

8. _____ (*They, Them*) were chasing each other across the field.

9. Then _____ (*they, them*) started chasing _____ (*she, her*).

10. _____ (*I, Me*) never saw _____ (*her, she*) run so fast.

11. _____ (*She, Her*) slid into second base just in time.

12. _____ (*We, Us*) all started jumping up and down.

13. A runner had scored for _____ (*we, us*)!

14. Those dogs made everyone look at _____ (*they, them*) instead of

    _____ (*her, she*).

15. _____ (*We, Us*) won, thanks to the dogs.

16. It was a relief for _____ (*me, I*).

Pronouns and Antecedents

An **antecedent** is the word a pronoun replaces or refers to. Every pronoun has an antecedent.

Example

Miners poured into California. **They** hoped to find gold.
("Miners" is the antecedent of "they.")

> **Directions** Underline the pronouns in the sentences below. Draw an arrow to each pronoun's antecedent. The first one has been done for you.

1. James Marshall got lucky. One morning he found gold in the river

   near his home.

2. Marshall didn't keep his secret for long.

3. By 1849, people from across the world heard the news. They headed

   for California.

4. Even the president got excited. California, he said, was a gold mine

   of riches.

5. The population of California grew quickly. In 1850, it became a state.

6. The people who got rich were the storekeepers. They sold high-priced

   food and pickaxes to the miners.

7. Most of the miners didn't find their pot of gold.

he	she	his	her	it	its	their

1. The band director helped students choose __*their*__ instruments.

2. Mr. Tweety brought many of _____ instruments to school.

3. Bill likes the trumpet for _____ loud, crisp sound.

4. Keisha chose the flute because _____ sounds like a bird.

5. Anne wants to play drums, but _____ mom may object.

6. Miguel thinks the slide trombone is amazing, but _____ also likes the French horn.

7. By next Tuesday, the students need to make _____ choices.

8. Mr. Tweety is keeping _____ fingers crossed.

9. Who will choose the tuba, or will _____ get passed by again?

NEXT STEP Do you play a musical instrument? Would you like to? Why or why not? Write your answers to these questions in two or three sentences. When you use a pronoun, draw an arrow to its antecedent.

....

....

....

....

Pronoun-Antecedent Agreement

Pronouns must agree with their antecedents. This means that both must be either singular or plural.

Examples

John walked his dog.
(Both "John" and the possessive pronoun "his" are singular.)

Eva and Cesar chose their cat carefully.
("Eva and Cesar," a compound subject, is plural, so the pronoun "their" is plural.)

Directions ▶ Draw an arrow from each underlined pronoun to its antecedent. If the pronoun does not agree with its antecedent, cross out the pronoun and write the correct one above it. The first one has been done for you.

1. Eva and Cesar wanted a pet and promised to take good care of ~~them~~. *it*

2. Their landlord doesn't allow dogs, but he does allow cats.

3. Eva and Cesar visited Positive Pets, an animal shelter in ~~his~~ *their* neighborhood.

4. The cages were filled with cats of all sizes and colors. ~~It~~ *They* napped.

5. Eva's attention was drawn to a lively kitten jumping against the sides of their cage.

6. The kitten seemed to be saying, "Get me out of here, please!"

7. Eva decided that was the kitten she wanted.

8. Cesar agreed, and he held the lively kitten on the way home.

Fill in the blank with the correct pronoun listed below. Draw an arrow back to the word that is the pronoun's antecedent. The first one has been done for you.

he	she	his	her	it	their	them

1. Many people get _____*their*_____ pets from animal shelters.

2. Shelters take in homeless animals and find good homes for _____.

3. Do animals from a shelter have something wrong with _____?

4. The pet owner has a problem, but _____ usually has nothing to do with the pet.

5. Mrs. Aguilar is moving and can't take _____ dog along.

6. My cousin is allergic and couldn't keep _____ cat.

7. Benji is a famous shelter dog. _____ became a Hollywood star.

8. Benji's story was exciting, and _____ helped many dogs get homes.

9. Many fine pets are waiting in shelters for _____ own homes.

NEXT STEP

Write one reason why someone might get a pet at a pet store instead of at a shelter or city pound. Write one reason why a shelter animal may be a good choice. Make sure your pronouns and antecedents agree.

....

....

....

....

Possessive Pronouns

Possessive pronouns show ownership. They often come before a noun, but not always.

Examples

Your cake is over there.
This cake is mine.

> **Directions** >> Underline all of the possessive pronouns in the following sentences. (The number at the end of each sentence tells whether that sentence has one or two possessive pronouns.) The first sentence has been done for you.

1. Did you bring <u>your</u> mom's pickles to the picnic? *(1)*

2. No, but I brought <u>her</u> ice-cream cake. *(1)*

3. Is the cake that is melting in the sun <u>hers</u> or <u>yours</u>? *(2)*

4. I'm afraid it's <u>mine</u>. *(1)*

5. That cake has definitely lost <u>its</u> shape. *(1)*

6. You should have used <u>his</u> cooler. *(1)*

7. I thought <u>his</u> was full of drinks. *(1)*

8. <u>Theirs</u> is full of sandwiches. *(1)*

9. <u>Ours</u> is empty. *(1)*

10. Is it too late to put <u>your</u> cake in <u>our</u> cooler? *(2)*

11. <u>Your</u> idea would have worked 30 minutes ago. *(1)*

12. I think <u>we</u> have donated our cake to the ants. *(1)*

13. It looks as if they have invited all <u>their</u> cousins to <u>our</u> picnic. *(2)*

Add possessive pronouns to the following sentences. Make your selection from the list below. The first one has been done for you.

my	your	his	her	its	our
their	mine	yours	hers	ours	

1. Michelle said the history report is ___hers___.

2. Tony finished _____ homework.

3. They are writing _____ poems.

4. Will she finish _____ on time?

5. Yes, _____ is nearly done.

6. We are working on _____ assignments together.

7. I have finished _____.

8. Will you work on _____ over the weekend?

9. Saturday is _____ favorite day of the week.

What is your favorite day of the week, and why? Write the answer in one or two complete sentences.

....

....

....

....

Indefinite Pronouns

Indefinite pronouns refer to people or things that are not named or known.

Examples

Does somebody have a good idea?
Neither of us can think of anything.

> **Directions** Underline all the indefinite pronouns in the sentences below. The first one has been done for you.

1. <u>Everyone</u> likes the movies.

2. <u>None</u> of us has money.

3. Does <u>anybody</u> have a different idea?

4. Let's think of <u>something</u> that is free.

5. <u>Several</u> of us will go to the park.

6. <u>Everything</u> else costs money.

7. <u>Somebody</u> said the library has a free movie.

8. <u>No one</u> knows what movie will be playing.

9. <u>A few</u> of us will go to the library.

10. <u>Others</u> will go to the zoo.

11. Can <u>anybody</u> think of a different choice?

12. <u>Anything</u> sounds like fun if we're together.

Add indefinite pronouns to the following script. Choose words from the list and use each word only once. The first sentence has been done for you.

somebody	either	any	most	others
both	something	many	one	anyone

1. **Salesperson:** Is _____anyone_____ home?

2. **Sabrina:** _____ of my parents are here.

3. **Salesperson:** I could talk to _____ of them.

4. **Sabrina:** Are you selling _____?

5. **Salesperson:** I have great deals on _____ of these magazines.

6. **Sabrina:** I don't think we want to buy _____ today.

7. **Salesperson:** _____ of my young customers like our coin-collecting magazines.

8. **Sabrina:** I'm not interested in _____ today.

9. **Salesperson:** I have _____ you might like.

10. **Sabrina:** I think I hear _____ calling me.

Read the script above with a partner, taking turns so each of you can read both parts. With a partner, try writing a script that uses some indefinite pronouns.

Action and Linking Verbs

Action verbs tell what the subject is doing.
Linking verbs connect the subject to a noun or
an adjective.

Examples

Trains **carry** passengers. ("Carry" is an action verb.)

He **is** a conductor.
(The linking verb "is" connects "he" to the noun, "conductor.")

She **became** nervous.
("Became" is a linking verb that connects "she" to the adjective "nervous.")

Directions > Underline the verb in each sentence. On the blank, identify each verb as "action" or "linking." The first one has been done for you.

_____ *linking* _____ 1. A locomotive <u>is</u> the engine on a train.

_____ 2. Locomotives pull the cars.

_____ 3. The biggest locomotives were huge.

_____ 4. Each of them tipped the scales at over 500,000 pounds.

_____ 5. The railroad built these monsters in the 1940s.

_____ 6. They called them "Big Boys."

_____ 7. The engines were powerful.

_____ 8. They almost looked scary.

_____ 9. They shook the ground.

_____ 10. Today, they are antiques in museums.

Read the story starter below. Fill in the blanks with action or linking verbs. You may use verbs from the list below or choose your own verbs. The first sentence has been done for you.

chugged	walked	carried	was	spun
looked	reached	caught	gave	were

1   The train _____gave_____ a long, lonely whistle. It _____

2   out of the station and headed into the cold, black night. A man with

3   a long overcoat and a wide-brimmed hat _____ stiffly through

4   the cars, keeping his balance. His eyes _____ narrow slits, and

5   his jaw _____ tight. Under his arm he _____ a

6   container with tiny airholes in the top. Just then, a young woman

7   with black glasses _____ up to the man in the overcoat. She

8   _____ furious. In an instant, she _____ him around.

9   She _____ for the container.

What do you think happened next? Write an ending for the story and share it with a partner or the whole class. Use both action and linking verbs.

....

....

....

Linking Verbs

A **linking verb** connects a subject to a noun or an adjective.

Examples

We are Americans.
(The linking verb "are" connects "we" to the noun "Americans.")

He feels excited.
(The linking verb "feels" connects "he" to the adjective "excited.")

> **Directions** » Underline each linking verb. Draw arrows between the words linked by each verb. The first one has been done for you.

1. The United States is a country of immigrants.

2. Today, many immigrants are Hispanics.

3. In the past, most immigrants were Europeans.

4. At first, many immigrants feel homesick.

5. Their new life is a puzzle in the beginning.

6. The cities in the United States seem strange.

7. In time, the immigrants become familiar with their new cities.

8. Everyone in America is an immigrant except Native Americans.

9. One fact remains true.

10. Immigrants are an important part of America.

Helping Verbs

A verb can be made up of one word or several words. When a verb is made of two or more verbs, the last verb is the main verb. A **helping verb** comes before a main verb and helps to state an action or show time.

Examples

I **have eaten** my sister's pancakes, and I **can eat** my dad's pancakes. ("Have" helps show the past tense of "eaten," and "can" helps state the action "eat.")

Helping Verbs					
can	did	had	have	must	will
could	do	has	may	should	would

Directions Underline the main verb in each of the following sentences. Then circle each helping verb. The first one has been done for you.

1. My dad (has) cooked pancakes on Saturdays for years.

2. He should follow a real recipe.

3. He did create his own recipe a long time ago.

4. Flat pancakes may please the dog.

5. I would like fluffier pancakes.

6. Maybe I will drop a few hints.

7. I can find a cookbook on the shelf.

8. He may get the idea.

9. We could try a new pancake recipe.

10. I could help Dad.

Verb Tenses 1

Different forms of a verb are used to show time. This is called the verb's **tense**. A **present tense** verb tells what is happening now. A **past tense** verb tells what has already happened.

Examples

I **am** sick. I **stay** in bed. (present tense)

I **was** sick. I **stayed** in bed. (past tense)

Directions ▶ On the line, write the tense ("present" or "past") of the underlined verb in each sentence. The first one has been done for you.

_____*past*_____ **1.** Yesterday, my throat <u>was</u> scratchy.

_____ **2.** My head <u>ached</u>.

_____ **3.** Mom <u>gave</u> me some medicine.

_____ **4.** It <u>tastes</u> like cherry-onion syrup.

_____ **5.** She <u>checks</u> in on me now and then.

_____ **6.** I <u>am</u> still sick, but not like yesterday.

_____ **7.** I <u>had</u> a fever yesterday.

_____ **8.** Luckily, I usually <u>recover</u> quickly.

Write one sentence in the past tense about a time when you were not feeling well. Then write one sentence in the present tense that tells how you feel now.

....

....

Verb Tenses 2

A verb's tense tells time. The **future tense** tells what will be happening. The word *will* is added before the main verb to make the future tense.

Examples

This year, I **grow** tomatoes. (present tense)

Next year, I **will grow** potatoes. (future tense)

> **Directions**   On the line, write the future tense of the verb in each of the following sentences. You may need to drop an "s" from the main verb. The first one has been done for you.

will plant   **1.** We plant a garden at school.

_____   **2.** The school buys us some seeds.

_____   **3.** They give us tomato and pepper plants.

_____   **4.** Sunshine beams down on the garden.

_____   **5.** Beans and peas climb the fence.

_____   **6.** We share the harvest.

_____   **7.** Everyone gets one pea and one bean.

_____   **8.** We plan a bigger garden for next year.

Pretend you are about to plant a small vegetable garden. Write a sentence telling a friend what you plan to grow.

....

....

Verb Tenses Review

Directions >> Underline the verb in each sentence. On the line, write whether the verb is "present," "past," or "future" tense.

_____ 1. When is Labor Day?

_____ 2. It falls on the first Monday in September.

_____ 3. Some schools begin classes the day after Labor Day.

_____ 4. It became a holiday in 1894.

_____ 5. This holiday honors workers.

_____ 6. "Labor" means "work."

_____ 7. Workers wanted an eight-hour workday.

_____ 8. They needed better pay.

_____ 9. They asked for safer workplaces.

_____ 10. We will not labor on Labor Day.

_____ 11. We will celebrate with a cookout.

_____ 12. Our neighbors will bring potato salad and watermelon.

_____ 13. We will play volleyball until dark.

_____ 14. School starts the next day.

_____ 15. We will not sleep late that morning!

Fill in the blanks with the tense of verb indicated (in parentheses).

1. Until recently, my stepdad _____ the night shift in a hospital.
   *(past tense of **work**)*

2. He _____ during the day, including Labor Day.
   *(past tense of **rest**)*

3. My mom _____ as a teacher.
   *(present tense of **work**)*

4. On Labor Day, she _____ her classroom ready.
   *(present tense of **get**)*

5. Now I _____ you about my Labor Day.
   *(future tense of **tell**)*

6. I _____ my younger brother get ready for school.
   *(past tense of **help**)*

7. He _____ and goofed off all morning.
   *(past tense of **play**)*

8. I _____ a load of clothes.
   *(past tense of **wash**)*

9. I _____ the dishes and _____ my room.
   *(past tense of **wash**)*   *(past tense of **clean**)*

10. Then my mom _____ from school.
    *(past tense of **call**)*

11. "I _____ carryout food from Casa de Tacos," she said.
    *(future tense of **bring**)*

12. "You _____ a treat!"
    *(present tense of **deserve**)*

Regular Verbs

Form the past tense of **regular verbs** by adding *ed*. Sometimes you may need to drop an *s* from the verb.

Examples

Present Tense:	marks	watch
Past Tense:	marked	watched

If a regular verb ends in *e*, just add *d* to form the past tense.

Present Tense:	dances	sneeze
Past Tense:	danced	sneezed

If a verb has one syllable and ends in a single consonant, here's what you do to change it to past tense: Double the final consonant and then add *ed*.

Present Tense:	taps	swat
Past Tense:	tapped	swatted

Directions ▶ On the blanks, write the past tense of these verbs. The first one has been done for you.

1. glide ____*glided*____
2. fit _____
3. attack _____
4. step _____
5. learn _____
6. hope _____
7. tug _____
8. wiggle _____

9. sip _____
10. pave _____
11. thank _____
12. stop _____
13. trade _____
14. travel _____
15. zap _____
16. fill _____

climbed

1   We <u>climb</u> the steps to the roller coaster and hand the man our

2   tickets. He smiles and waves us into the next car. Once inside, we

3   fasten our safety belts and giggle. Slowly we chug up the first hill.

4   At the top, we stop for one long, dreadful moment. We stare at all

5   the people on the ground, as small as ants. Then, with a jolt, we

6   plunge down the hill and whip around the track. All too soon, we

7   arrive back at the starting point. We stagger down the steps and

8   look at each other. "One more time!" we scream, and we race back

9   up the stairs.

Read the new version of the story aloud to a partner. Try reading the story to each other again. This time change all the verbs to the future tense.

Irregular Verbs

Irregular verbs don't follow a simple pattern when their tense is changed. However, with enough practice, they will sound right to your ear. Here are some examples:

Examples

Present Tense	Past Tense	Past Tense with have, has, or had
break	broke	broken
fall	fell	fallen

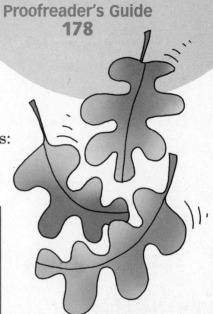

> **Directions** Fill in the missing forms of the following irregular verbs. See the chart on page 178. The first one has been done for you.

Present Tense	Past Tense	Past Tense with have, has, or had
1. begin	*began*	*begun*
2. catch		
3. do		
4. drink		
5. fly		
6. know		
7. ride		
8. run		
9. set		
10. write		

Directions

Look at the chart on page 178. On the line, write the correct past tense form of the irregular verb (in parentheses) in each sentence. The first one has been done for you.

1. We _____*went*_____ (*go*) to our basketball game last week.

2. My team _____ (*lead*) for most of the game.

3. Several times I _____ (*steal*) the ball.

4. I had _____ (*do*) my best.

5. Then I _____ (*run*) down the court with the ball.

6. I _____ (*throw*) it into the air.

7. I had _____ (*make*) a basket from 18 feet!

8. Oh, no! I had _____ (*sink*) the ball in the wrong basket.

9. I _____ (*fight*) back tears.

10. The coach _____ (*catch*) up to me after the game.

11. He _____ (*give*) me the thumbs-up sign.

12. Then I _____ (*know*) I would be all right again.

In one short sentence, write what you think the coach said to the player who made a basket for the other team. See if you can use an irregular verb correctly.

....

....

Singular and Plural Verbs 1

The subject of a sentence can be singular (one) or plural (more than one). **Verbs** can also be singular or plural. The tricky part is getting the subject to "agree" with the verb. Both must be either singular or plural.

Examples

The wind **blows**. ("Wind" is singular, so the singular verb "blows" agrees with it. Singular action verbs usually end in "s.")

The waves **roll**. ("Waves" is plural, so the plural verb "roll" agrees with it. Plural verbs usually do not end in "s.")

Note: The words "I" and "you" need plural action verbs.

Directions ▶ Underline the verb in parentheses that agrees with the subject of the sentence. The first one has been done for you.

1. Many strange creatures (*come*, *comes*) from the sea.

2. I (*have*, *has*) seen some of them.

3. We (*visit*, *visits*) the aquarium each summer.

4. My mom (*love*, *loves*) the sea.

5. Too bad she (*live*, *lives*) in Iowa.

6. My brother (*like*, *likes*) the sharks and dolphins.

7. I (*watch*, *watches*) jellyfish in a dark room.

8. They (*wiggle*, *wiggles*) mysteriously through the water.

9. I (*study*, *studies*) them for a long time.

On the line in each sentence, write the singular or plural form of the verb (in parentheses). Your verb must agree with the subject. The first one has been done for you.

1. Humans _____walk_____ (*walk*) on two legs.

2. Most animals _____ (*move*) on four legs.

3. An octopus _____ (*have*) eight legs.

4. These sea creatures _____ (*look*) creepy to me.

5. Suckers _____ (*cover*) their legs.

6. These suction cups _____ (*capture*) small fish.

7. An octopus _____ (*do*) not run on its eight legs.

8. This animal _____ (*squeeze*) itself into the smallest holes.

9. When in danger, these creatures _____ (*squirt*) ink.

10. This action _____ (*confuse*) their enemies.

11. The ink _____ (*cloud*) the water.

12. Just like that, the octopus _____ (*escape*).

Draw an octopus or another sea animal. In one sentence tell what you think is most unusual about this creature.

....

....

Singular and Plural Verbs 2

Some sentences have compound subjects. This means that the sentence has two or more subjects. A compound subject joined by *and* needs a plural verb.

My mom and dad **love** bargains.
("Mom and dad," a compound subject, is plural, so the plural verb "love" agrees with it.)

A compound subject joined by *or* may need either a singular or a plural verb. Here's the way to know which verb to use: The verb must agree with the subject that is closest to it.

Stylish clothes or a new necklace **makes** my day.
("Necklace" is singular and needs the singular verb "makes.")

Stylish clothes or new necklaces **make** my day.
("Necklaces" is plural, so the plural verb "make" is correct.)

Directions ▸ In the following sentences, circle the word "and" or "or." On the line, write the form of the verb in parentheses that agrees with the compound subject. The first one has been done for you.

1. My sister (and) I ___**need**___ (*need*) new clothes.

2. Grandma or Mom usually _____ (*drive*) us to the store.

3. My sister and I _____ (*like*) new clothes.

4. My brothers and my dad _____ (*stay*) home.

5. Shops or malls _____ (*bore*) them.

6. My dad or my brothers _____ (*unload*) the car.

7. Mom and my sister _____ (*are*) tired.

8. My brothers or my dad _____ (*make*) dinner.

Add a verb and some other words to complete the following sentences. Use present-tense action verbs that are one word only, such as those from the list below. Make sure the verbs you choose agree with their subjects. The first one has been done for you.

plan	run	climb	eat
toss	go	play	bow

1. My friends and I _eat lots of pizza_ _____ .

2. Crickets or a spider _____ .

3. The teachers or the students _____ .

4. The singers and dancer _____ .

5. Tapes, CD's, or the radio _____ .

6. My neighbors and friends _____ .

7. Hot chocolate and donuts _____ .

"Be" Verbs

"Be" wise and learn how to use the **"be" verbs** correctly. The forms of "be" are either linking verbs or helping verbs. Read the following patterns.

Linking Verbs

Present Tense: I **am** hungry.   He **is** hungry.   We **are** hungry.

Past Tense: I **was** hungry.   He **was** hungry.   We **were** hungry.

Helping Verbs

Present Tense: I **am** drinking.   She **is** drinking.   They **are** drinking.

Past Tense: I **was** drinking.   She **was** drinking.   They **were** drinking.

> **Directions** On the line, write the form of the "be" verb that agrees with the subject. (The tense to use is in parentheses.) The first one has been done for you.

1. I _____ *am* _____ (*present tense*) a big fan of peanuts.

2. Sometimes, a peanut _____ (*present tense*) called a "goober."

3. Peanuts _____ (*present tense*) not nuts.

4. Some people say that I _____ (*present tense*) a nut.

5. Nuts _____ (*present tense*) actually seeds!

6. We _____ (*past tense*) eating at a restaurant the other day.

7. Peanut shells _____ (*past tense*) scattered all over the floor.

8. They _____ (*past tense*) broken.

9. It _____ (*past tense*) a big mess.

10. There _____ (*present tense*) nothing like salted peanuts.

Verb Review

This activity reviews subject-verb agreement.

> **Directions** >> In the following story, cross out any verb that does not agree with its subject. Write the correct verb above it. If the verb does agree, write "C" above it to show that it is correct.

1   Every summer our family has a reunion. We drives all night

2   from Michigan to my aunt and uncle's farm in North Carolina. Aunt

3   Lyn always give us a good, old-fashioned country breakfast. The kids

4   and my grandma does the dishes. Then we bring out the horseshoes

5   and play. During the rest of the day, the adults sits around in lawn

6   chairs and talk nonstop. My cousins and I run off to explore the farm.

7   We ride the old pony and swings on a big rubber tire in a tree. The

8   farm be the best place in the world for hide-and-seek. Amy and I

9   hides from the little kids in a stack of sweet-smelling hay. In the

10   afternoon, Uncle Art roasts a whole pig. At night, everybody watch

11   home movies from last year's reunion. As Amy and I fall asleep, we is

12   always plotting what to do the next day.

Common and Proper Adjectives

Adjectives are words that describe nouns or pronouns. They tell *what kind, how many,* or *which one.* Adjectives usually come right before the words they describe. Sometimes they follow linking verbs.

Examples

> We walked into the thick, dark forest. (before a noun)
>
> She was curious. (after a linking verb)

Most adjectives are not capitalized. They are called **common adjectives**. Adjectives that are capitalized are called **proper adjectives**.

> At a Minnesota lake, we had a picnic in a lovely park.
> ("Minnesota" is a proper adjective; "lovely" is a common adjective.)

> **Directions**   Underline each adjective in the following sentences. Draw an arrow to the noun it describes. Then write "PA" above each proper adjective. The first one has been done for you.

1. Theodore Roosevelt was a famous president.

2. He loved the North Dakota badlands. *(PA)*

3. One summer he camped in a California forest. *(PA)*

4. He slept under the sequoia trees.

5. He wrote about his wonderful trip.

6. Roosevelt helped create national forests.

7. Once he saved a small bear from hunters.

8. A Washington newspaper printed a cartoon about the bear. *(PA)*

9. Soon, toy bears were being called "teddy bears."

Add adjectives to the following sentences. The first one has been done for you.

1. Bears are _____*wild*_____ animals.

2. They have _____ bodies and _____ jaws.

3. Through the _____ winter, they hibernate.

4. When spring comes, they are _____.

5. Bears have a _____ sense of smell.

6. This helps them find _____ food to eat.

7. Bears have _____ appetites.

8. Campers should lock up food in _____ places.

9. Bears are not _____ dinner guests.

Pretend you are a game warden in bear country. Use powerful adjectives on a sign that grabs campers' attention and warns them about bears.

Forms of Adjectives

Adjectives have three forms:

Examples

A **positive adjective** does not make a comparison.

New York is a large city.

A **comparative adjective** compares two things.

Mexico City is larger than New York.

A **superlative adjective** compares three or more things.

Tokyo is the largest city in the world.

More or *most* (or *less* and *least*) are sometimes used with longer adjectives (instead of adding *er* or *est*) when making comparisons.

Greenland is the least crowded country in the world.

 **Directions** In the following paragraph, underline the correct choice of the two adjective forms in parentheses. The first one has been done for you.

1   What are the (*more popular*, *most popular*) cereals in the

2   world? They don't come in (*colorful*, *more colorful*) boxes. They

3   aren't (*sweet*, *sweeter*) than candy. They aren't advertised as the

4   (*greatest*, *most greatest*) thing since handheld video games. These

5   cereals don't promise to make you (*healthy*, *healthier*) than other

6   people or (*more energetic*, *most energetic*) than the rest of your

7   friends. Real cereal is a form of grass! It is (*cheaper*, *more cheaper*)

8   than boxed cereal. In China, the (*bigger*, *biggest*) country in the

9   world, people eat rice every day. Rice, corn, and wheat are the (*more*

10 *important*, *most important*) cereals in the world.

In the sentences below, fill in the lines with the correct adjective forms. The first one has been done for you.

1. The temperature today is hot. Yesterday was ____*hotter*____ than today. Tomorrow will be the _____ day of the week.

2. Rabbits are fast. Zebras are _____ than rabbits. Cheetahs are the world's _____ animal.

3. Football is an exciting sport, but I think hockey is _____, and basketball is the _____ sport of all.

4. Molly is a tall fifth grader, but Jason is _____ , and Tamika is the _____ person in our class.

5. I like loud music. My brother likes even _____ music than I do, but our neighbor likes the _____ music in the world!

6. Toastie Rice is delicious. Crispy Flakes is _____ than Toastie Rice. A+ Apple Crunch is the _____ cereal of all.

Name your own cereal and give it special qualities. In three sentences, tell why your cereal is better than any other cereal.

....

....

....

Irregular Adjectives

Some comparative and superlative adjectives are completely different words than the positive form.

Positive	Comparative	Superlative
bad	worse	worst
good	better	best
many	more	most
little	less	least

Directions ⟩⟩ Underline the correct adjective forms in the following paragraph. The first one has been done for you.

1   That was the (*worst*, *worsest*) movie I ever saw. The actors

2   were (*good*, *better*), but the story was (*bad*, *worse*). (*More*, *Many*)

3   people left early. I took a (*less*, *little*) nap in the middle. When I

4   woke up, the movie had only gotten (*worse*, *worser*). The special

5   effects were (*less interesting*, *least interesting*) than the credits. I

6   could have had a (*gooder*, *better*) time at home. The only (*better*,

7   *good*) thing was that we paid (*little*, *less*) money than we would have

8   paid at night. The (*good*, *best*) part was seeing the words "The End."

What do you like best in a movie? Give your answer in two sentences.

....

....

Compound Adjectives

Compound adjectives are made of two words. Sometimes these words have a hyphen between them. Sometimes they do not.

Examples

a **half-baked** potato   **superhuman** power

Directions ▶ Match each compound adjective in the first column with the best choice from the second column. Write the correct letter on the line. The first one has been done for you.

___b___ 1. a <u>four-sided</u> shape   **a.** pollution

___h___ 2. a <u>two-ton</u> truck   **b.** a square

___f___ 3. a <u>self-centered</u> person   **c.** hammers, nails, paint

___e___ 4. a <u>homesick</u> camper   **d.** an animal with light fur

___c___ 5. a <u>hardware</u> store   **e.** misses home

___d___ 6. a <u>white-haired</u> dog   **f.** doesn't think of others

___g___ 7. a <u>six-inch</u> ruler   **g.** a short measuring tool

___a___ 8. a <u>worldwide</u> problem   **h.** 4,000 pounds

NEXT STEP Write a phrase with a compound adjective for (1) shoes that have high heels, (2) a monster with five heads, (3) a girl with brown eyes, and (4) a bike with three wheels. Don't forget the hyphens!

1. _____   3. _____

2. _____   4. _____

© Great Source. Copying is prohibited.

128 Adjectives

Using Adverbs

Adverbs are words that describe verbs. They tell *how, when,* or *where.*

Examples

I looked **nervously** at the sky. (tells "how")

The sun will shine **tomorrow**. (tells "when")

We ran **inside**. (tells "where")

Directions > Underline the adverbs in these sentences. On the line, write whether the adverb tells *how, when,* or *where*. The first one has been done for you.

how	**1.** The day started <u>beautifully</u>.
everywhere	**2.** Blue skies were <u>everywhere</u>.
Suddenly	**3.** <u>Suddenly</u>, the temperature dropped.
quickly	**4.** The sky <u>quickly</u> became dark.
carefully	**5.** We listened to the TV <u>carefully</u>.
nearby	**6.** A tornado had been spotted <u>nearby</u>.
downstairs	**7.** We ran <u>downstairs</u> to our basement.
anxiously	**8.** We waited <u>anxiously</u>.
Finally	**9.** <u>Finally</u>, the storm passed.
upside down	**10.** Our grill landed <u>upside down</u> on the roof!

carefully	*away*	*quickly*	*often*
downstairs	*around*	*down*	*violently*

1   Tornadoes are _____ **sometimes** _____ called twisters because

2   they have winds that twist _____. These winds

3   form a funnel that spins _____ in a fast circle,

4   like a huge top. If the bottom of that funnel ever touches

5   _____ on the ground, watch out! Tornado winds

6   _____ reach 200 miles per hour. In the "tornado

7   belt," experts scan the skies _____ for tornadoes.

8   When they spot a tornado, they _____ send out a

9   warning: Go _____ to the lowest point in your

10 house! Stay _____ from windows!

What do you think is the most important thing to remember in any emergency? Answer this question in one or two sentences. Use an adverb in each.

....

....

....

130   Adverbs

Forms of Adverbs

Like adjectives, adverbs have three different forms:

Examples

A **positive** adverb does not make a comparison.
I read carefully and wrote fast.

A **comparative** adverb compares two things.
He read more carefully and wrote faster than I did.
(Add "more" or "less" to adverbs that end in "ly."
Add "er" to short adverbs.)

A **superlative** adverb compares three or more things.
She read most carefully and wrote the fastest of all of us.
(Add "most" or "least" to adverbs that end in "ly." Add "est" to short adverbs.)

Some adverbs, like those in the chart, are irregular. Be careful not to use the adjective *good* as an adverb. Remember, adverbs describe verbs.

Positive	Comparative	Superlative
well	**better**	**best**
badly	**worse**	**worst**

Directions In the following paragraph, underline the correct adverb in parentheses. The first one has been done for you.

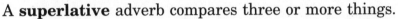

1   I learn math (*more easily*, *most easily*) than I memorize facts. I

2   did not do (*good*, *well*) on our state capitals test. My friend did

3   (*badly*, *worse*) than I did, even though she finished (*most quickly*,

4   *more quickly*). Enrico scored the (*higher*, *highest*) in our class. He

5   answered every question (*correctly*, *correct*). I answered (*poor*,

6   *poorly*) on the New England states. Next time, I will perform (*better*,

7   *best*) than I did this time. You can't be a genius at everything!

In the sentences below, fill in the lines with the correct adverb forms. The first one has been done for you.

1. Peas grow well in that spot, but beans grow ____*better*____ than the

   peas, and lettuce grows _____ of all.

2. Nena behaved badly, but Gina behaved _____ than her,

   and Tina behaved the _____ of the three girls.

3. Tara held the safety strap tightly. Mayra held it _____

   _____ than Tara did, and Gena held it the

   _____ of all.

4. Tom finished his work quickly, but Alex finished _____

   _____ than Tom did, and Ted finished

   the _____ of all.

5. Haley performed well at the music contest, but Laura did

   _____ than Haley did. Jana performed the

   _____ of all the contestants.

Write three sentences using *well, better*, and *best* as adverbs. Remember, an adverb describes a verb.

....

....

....

Using Prepositions

Prepositions can show direction or position. A preposition is the first word in a prepositional phrase. The phrase also includes a noun or pronoun (the object) and any modifiers. A list of common prepositions can be found on page 182.

Examples

In the winter, we go sledding.

("In" is the preposition at the beginning of this phrase.)

We zip through the snow.

(This prepositional phrase begins with the preposition "through.")

> **Directions**   In each sentence below, circle any preposition. Then underline the whole prepositional phrase. The first one has been done for you.

1. Two men climbed (up) a mountain.

2. Then they (headed) for their camp.

3. They (came) to a crevasse.

4. A crevasse is a deep, wide crack (in) an ice sheet.

5. The men, who were joined (by) a rope, stopped.

6. One man tried leaping (across) the crevasse, but he slipped and fell.

7. Suddenly, he felt a firm tug (at) his waist.

8. He dangled (in) midair.

9. Then he swung (into) the ice wall.

10. He cut steps (from) the ice and started climbing.

11. This is one (of) the stories told by men who climbed Mt. Everest.

Using Interjections

An **interjection** is a word that shows strong emotion or excitement.

Examples

Yeah!   **Wait!** I'm coming, too!   **Wow,** that's great!

Directions ▸ Write a different interjection on each line in the following sentences. The first one has been done for you.

Rah	Well	Help	Watch out	Look out
Wow	Stop	Oh no	Oh dear	Oh my

1. Everyone at school cheered. _____Hurray_____! We had made the play-offs! The bleachers were jammed with fans. When the team came on the field, the crowd roared. _____!

2. _____, what can I say? I tried my best, but I guess I did not study hard enough for the test. _____!

3. _____! Don't go in there! There is a sleeping bear in that cave! _____ , Carlo is going in there.

4. Are you moving away, Angie? _____, that makes me sad.

Choose one of the sentences above, and write two or three sentences to continue the story. Use interjections to show excitement.

....

....

Using Conjunctions 1

Conjunctions are words that connect other words, sentence parts, or entire sentences. The most common conjunctions are *and, but, or, nor, for, so,* and *yet.*

Examples

The grasshopper **and** the ant are characters in a famous story. ("And" connects two subjects.)

The ant grew her own food **and** stored it away. ("And" connects two phrases.)

Directions	Underline all the conjunctions in the following story. There are eight in all. The first one has been underlined for you.

The North Wind and the Sun

1   The North Wind <u>and</u> the Sun argued about who was more

2   powerful. Was the force of the Wind or the heat of the Sun stronger?

3   They decided to have a contest. They would find a woman walking

4   outside, and whoever could get the coat off her first would win.

5   The North Wind thought that he could blow the woman's coat

6   off. Swirls of air spun around her, yet her coat stayed on. The Wind

7   blew harder and harder at the woman, but she kept wrapping her

8   coat tighter around her body to keep the cold away.

9   Then it was the Sun's turn. The Sun shone down brightly on the

10   woman. She felt warmer and warmer, so she ended up taking off her

11   coat. The Sun had won the contest.

Using Conjunctions 2

What is a **subordinating conjunction**? It is a special kind of conjunction that joins sentences. When you use a subordinating conjunction to begin part of a sentence, you need the other part in order for it to make sense.

Two Sentences: The men were blind.
They could "see" things with their other senses.

Combined: Although the men were blind, they could "see" things with their other senses.

See page 183 for a list of subordinating conjunctions. Just remember this: A group of words that begins with one of these conjunctions cannot stand alone as a sentence.

> **Directions** — Underline the subordinating conjunctions in this story. There are six in all. The first one has been done for you.

The Blind Men and the Elephant

1 Six men were arguing about what an elephant looked like,

2 though all six were blind. They decided to go on a field trip and "see"

3 for themselves, since they couldn't agree. When they got to the

4 elephant, the first man felt its side. He said, "The elephant is like a

5 wall!" Then the second man touched the elephant's leg, while the

6 third man grabbed its tail. The second man said, "The elephant is

7 like a tree!" The third man said, "No! The elephant is like a snake!"

8 And so it went. After each man had his turn, the six blind men began

9 to argue. Each was sure he knew the truth because he had felt a part

10 of the elephant.

Parts of Speech Review 1

Directions ▶ Each list below contains words that are the same part of speech. Read each list and label it with the correct part of speech.

noun   *verb*   *adverb*   *preposition*

pronoun   *adjective*   *conjunction*   *interjection*

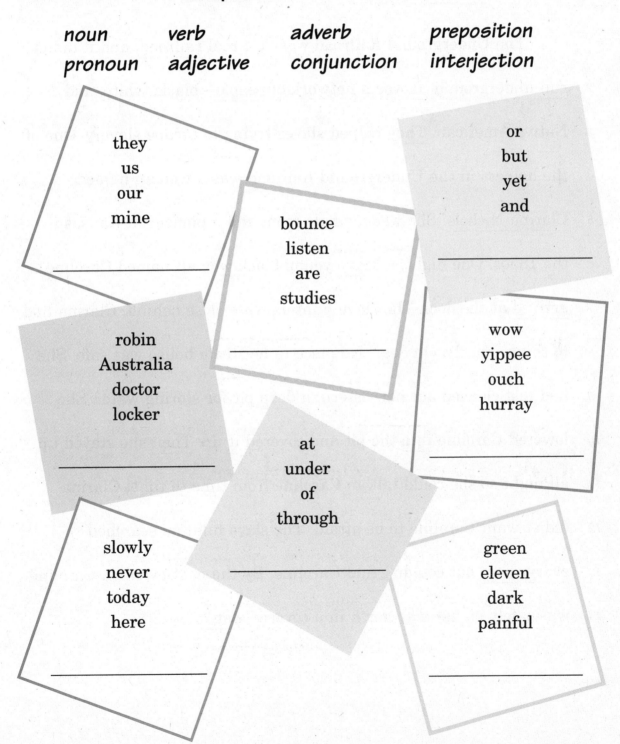

they
us
our
mine

_____

or
but
yet
and

_____

bounce
listen
are
studies

_____

robin
Australia
doctor
locker

_____

wow
yippee
ouch
hurray

_____

at
under
of
through

_____

slowly
never
today
here

_____

green
eleven
dark
painful

_____

Parts of Speech
Review 2

Directions ▶ Below is a true story about the Underground Railroad. Above each underlined word, write what part of speech the word is.

1   The Underground Railroad wasn't a real <u>railroad</u>, and it didn't

2   <u>run</u> underground. <u>It</u> was a network of <u>people</u>—black, white, and

3   Native American. <u>They</u> helped slaves trying to escape slavery. One of

4   the helpers in the Underground Railroad was a woman named

5   <u>Clarina Nichols</u>. She was a single mom and a pioneer in Kansas in

6   the 1850s. One night, a <u>brave</u> young black woman named Caroline

7   <u>arrived</u> at the door. The slave hunters were close <u>behind</u>. Clarina had

8   to think quickly. <u>Oh dear</u>! No place in her little house was safe. She

9   had just cleaned out her cistern, a <u>deep</u> pit for storing water. She

10   lowered Caroline <u>into</u> the pit and covered it up. <u>Then</u> she stayed up

11   all night <u>so</u> she could talk to Caroline from time to time. Clarina

12   didn't <u>want</u> Caroline to be afraid. The slave hunters searched

13   <u>everywhere</u> but couldn't find Caroline. By the next evening, Caroline

14   was safely on her way north in a covered <u>wagon</u>.

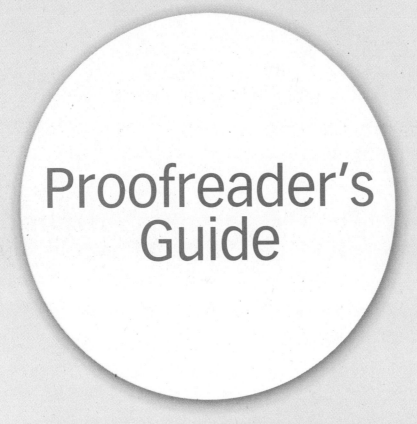

Proofreader's Guide

The following pages present basic rules and examples for punctuation, mechanics, usage, spelling, and grammar. Check here whenever you have an editing and proofreading question.

Marking Punctuation

Period

A **period** is used to end a sentence. It is also used after initials, as a decimal point, and after abbreviations.

At the End of a Sentence	Use a period to end a sentence that makes a statement, a command, or a request. **Taro won the fishing contest.** (statement) **Take his picture.** (command) **Please pass the bait.** (request)
After an Initial	Place a period after an initial in a person's name. **Susan B. Anthony A. A. Milne**
As a Decimal	Use a period as a decimal point and to separate dollars and cents. **Robert is 99.9 percent sure that the bus pass costs $2.50.**
After Abbreviations	Use a period after each part of an abbreviation. **Mr. Mrs. Ms. Jr. Dr. Ph.D. U.S.A.**
After Final Abbreviations	Use only one period for an abbreviation at the end of a sentence. **When Josie is nervous, she whistles, wiggles, winks, etc.**

Question Mark

A **question mark** is used after a direct question (an interrogative sentence) and to show doubt about the correctness of something.

Direct Question	Place a question mark at the end of a direct question. **Do you want to visit other galaxies?**
To Show Doubt	Place a question mark in parentheses to show that you aren't sure a fact is correct. **The ship arrived in Boston on July 23 (?), 1652.**

Exclamation Point

To Express Strong Feeling	An **exclamation point** is used to express strong feeling. It may be placed after a word, a phrase, or a sentence. **Surprise!** (word) **Happy birthday!** (phrase) **Wait for me!** (sentence) TIP: Never use double exclamation points.

Comma

Commas are used to keep words and ideas from running together. They tell your reader where to pause, which makes your writing easier to read.

Between Items in a Series

Place commas between words, phrases, or clauses in a series. (A *series* is three items or more in a row.)

Nona likes pepperoni, pineapple, and olives on her pizza. (words)

During the summer I read mysteries, rode my bike, and played basketball. (phrases)

In Dates and Addresses

Use commas to separate items in addresses and dates.

We had a family picnic on July 4, 2003, at Montrose Beach.

My new address is 3344 South First Street, Atlanta, GA 30200.

TIP: Do not use a comma between the state and ZIP code.

To Keep Numbers Clear

Place commas between hundreds, thousands, millions, and so on.

Rodney's car has 200,000 miles on it. He wants to sell it for $1,000.

TIP: Commas are not used in years: 1776, 1999, 2010.

To Set Off Interruptions

Use commas to set off a word, phrase, or clause that interrupts the main thought of a sentence.

As it turned out, however, Rodney sold the car for $250.

To Set Off Dialogue

Set off the exact words of the speaker from the rest of the sentence with a comma.

The stranded frog replied, "I'm just waiting for the toad truck."

No comma is needed when *reporting* rather than *repeating* what a speaker said.

The stranded frog said he was waiting for the toad truck.

Between Two Independent Clauses

Use a comma between two independent clauses that are joined by coordinating conjunctions *and, but, or, nor, for, so,* and *yet.*

Aquarium workers love animals, so they rescue hurt ones.

The team rehabilitated the sick sea lion pups, and then they released them.

TIP: Do not connect two independent clauses with a comma only. (See page 166 for more information about independent clauses.)

In Letter Writing

Place a comma after the salutation, or greeting, in a friendly letter and after the closing in all letters.

Dear Uncle Jim, (greeting)   **Sincerely,** (closing)

To Separate Adjectives	Use commas to separate two or more adjectives that equally modify a noun.
	I like the feel of cold, salty water when I go wading.
	TIP: Use these tests to discover if adjectives modify equally:
	• Switch the order of the adjectives; if the sentence is still clear, the adjectives modify equally.
	• Insert *and* between the adjectives; if the sentence reads well, use a comma when *and* is omitted.
To Set Off Interjections	Use a comma to separate an interjection or a weak exclamation from the rest of the sentence.
	Wow, look at that sunrise! **Hey, we're up early!**
To Set Off Appositives	Use commas to set off appositives. An *appositive* is a word or phrase that renames the noun or pronoun before it.
	My father, a great cook, makes the best egg rolls in town. (an appositive phrase)
To Set Off Introductory Phrases and Clauses	Use a comma to separate a long phrase or clause that comes before the main part of the sentence.
	After checking my knee pads, I started off. (phrase)
	If you practice often, skating is easy. (clause)

Colon

A **colon** can introduce a list or draw attention to information that follows. Colons are also used in business letters and between the numbers expressing time.

To Introduce a List	Use a colon to introduce a list following a complete sentence.
	Snorkelers need the right equipment: fins, masks, and life belts.
	When introducing a list, the colon often comes after summary words like *the following* or *these things*.
	Scuba divers often see the following: barracuda, eels, turtles, and jellyfish.
	TIP: It is <u>incorrect</u> to use a colon after a verb or a preposition.
	I made a salad of: lettuce, tomatoes, cucumber, and dressing. (The colon is <u>incorrectly</u> used after the preposition *of*.)
	My favorite salad toppings include: bacon, raisins, sunflower seeds, croutons. (The colon is <u>incorrectly</u> used after the verb *include*.)

After a Salutation	Place a colon after the salutation of a business letter.
	Dear Ms. Koplin: **Dear Chairperson:**
Between Numbers in Time	Place a colon between the parts of a number indicating time.
	The race begins at 1:30 p.m.
	I'll meet you at 12:00 noon.

Hyphen

A **hyphen** is used to divide a word at the end of a line. Hyphens are also used to join or create new words.

To Divide a Word	Use a hyphen to divide a word when you run out of room at the end of a line. Divide words only between syllables. (The word *en-vi-ron-ment* can be divided in three places.)
	John McConnell showed concern for the natural envi-
	ronment by founding Earth Day.
	TIP: Here are some other guidelines for hyphenating words:
	● Never divide a one-syllable word: **showed, great.**
	● Never divide a one-letter syllable from the rest of the word: **i-dentity.**
	● Never divide contractions: **haven't, shouldn't.**
In Compound Words	Use a hyphen in certain compound words.
	well-done **baby-sitter** **off-key**
Between Numbers in Fractions	Use a hyphen between the numbers in a fraction.
	One-fourth of the group gobbled seven-eighths
	of the cake!
To Form an Adjective	Use a hyphen to join two or more words that work together to form a single adjective before a noun.
	blue-green sea **sister-proof closet**
	big-grin smile **knee-worn jeans**
To Create New Words	Use a hyphen to form new words beginning with the prefixes *self, ex, great, all,* and *half.* A hyphen is also used with suffixes such as *free* and *elect.*
	self-made **all-purpose** **fat-free**
	great-aunt **half-baked** **president-elect**
To Join Letters and Words	Use a hyphen to join a letter to a word.
	T-shirt **T-ball** **X-ray** **e-mail** **U-turn**

Apostrophe

An **apostrophe** is used to form plurals, to form contractions, to show that a letter or letters have been left out of a word, or to show possession.

To Join Letters and Words

Use an apostrophe to show that one or more letters have been left out to form a contraction. Here are some common contractions.

Common Contractions

couldn't (could not)	haven't (have not)	she's (she is)
didn't (did not)	I'll (I will)	they'll (they will)
doesn't (does not)	isn't (is not)	they're (they are)
don't (do not)	it's (it is; it has)	wouldn't (would not)
hasn't (has not)	I've (I have)	you'd (you would)

To Form Plurals

Use an apostrophe and *s* to form the plural of a letter, a number, or a sign.

A's (letter)   8's (number)   +'s (sign)

In Place of Omitted Numbers or Letters

Use an apostrophe to show that one or more letters or numbers have been left out.

class of '99 (*19* is left out)

fixin' to go (*g* is left out)

To Form Singular Possessives

Add an apostrophe and *s* to make the possessive form of most singular nouns.

My sister's hobby is jazz dancing.

When a singular noun ends with an *s* or *z* sound, you may form the possessive by adding just an apostrophe.

Lucas' hobby is collecting pencil stubs.

Except: When a singular noun is a one-syllable word, add both an apostrophe and an *s*.

Gus's father took him fishing.

To Form Plural Possessives

Add just an apostrophe to make the possessive form of plural nouns ending in *s*.

the girls' logrolling team

For plural nouns not ending in *s*, add an apostrophe and *s*.

children's book

Quotation Marks

Quotation marks are used to enclose the exact words of the speaker, to show that words are used in a special way, and to punctuate titles.

To Set Off Direct Quotations	Place quotation marks before and after the spoken words. "Rosa Parks is a true American hero," the teacher reminded her students.
Placement of Punctuation	Put periods and commas inside quotation marks. Trev said, "Let's make tuna sandwiches." "Sounds good," said Rich. Place question marks or exclamation points inside the quotation marks when they punctuate the quotation; place them outside when they punctuate the main sentence. "Will we have tuna and apples?" asked Trev. "Yes!" replied Rich. Did you hear Mom say, "We're out of pickles"?
For Special Words	Quotation marks may be used to set apart a word that is being discussed. The word "scrumptious" is hard to spell.
To Punctuate Titles	Place quotation marks around titles of songs, poems, short stories, essays, and chapters of books. Also use quotation marks with articles found in magazines, newspapers, encyclopedias, or electronic sources. (See page 147.) "America the Beautiful" (song) "McBroom Tells the Truth" (short story) "Water, Water Everywhere" (chapter) **TIP:** When you write a title, capitalize the first word, the last word, and every word in between except for articles (*a, an, the*), short prepositions (*by, for, with*), and coordinating conjunctions (*and, or, but*).

Italics is a printer's term for type that is slightly slanted. Italics is used for titles and special words. *Note:* In handwritten material, each word or letter that should be in italics is <u>underlined</u>. If you use a computer, you should use italics.

For Titles

Use italics (or underlining) for titles of plays, books, newspapers, magazines, television programs, movies (videos), record albums (cassettes and CD's), DVD's, and other complete works.

> *The Wiz* OR <u>The Wiz</u> (play)
>
> *Exploring an Ocean Tide Pool* (book)
>
> *Pinky and the Brain* (television program)
>
> *The Prince of Egypt* (movie)

For Specific Words

Use italics (or underlining) to indicate names of aircraft and ships.

> *Discovery* OR <u>Discovery</u> (spacecraft)
>
> *Merrimac* OR <u>Merrimac</u> (Civil War ship)

Use italics (or underlining) to indicate foreign words.

> *E pluribus unum*, meaning "one out of many," is written on many U.S. coins.

Use italics (or underlining) to indicate words discussed as words, rather than for their meaning.

> The word *freedom* means different things to different people.

Punctuation Marks

é	Accent		. . .	Ellipsis
'	Apostrophe		!	Exclamation Point
*	Asterisk		-	Hyphen
[ ]	Brackets		( )	Parentheses
∧	Caret		.	Period
:	Colon		?	Question Mark
,	Comma		" "	Quotation Marks
—	Dash		;	Semicolon
/	Diagonal/Slash		_	Underscore

Editing for Mechanics

Capitalization

Proper Nouns and Proper Adjectives	Capitalize all proper nouns and proper adjectives. A proper noun names a specific person, place, thing, or idea. A proper adjective is formed from a proper noun.

Proper Nouns:

Beverly Cleary   **Golden Gate Bridge**

Utah Jazz   **Thanksgiving**

Proper Adjectives:

American citizen   **Chicago skyline**   **New Jersey shore**

Names of People

Capitalize the names of people and also the initials or abbreviations that stand for those names.

John Steptoe   **Harriet Tubman**
C. S. Lewis   **Sacagawea**

Words Used as Names

Capitalize words such as *mother, father, aunt,* and *uncle* when these words are used as names.

Ask Mother what we're having for lunch. ("Mother" is used as a name; you could use her first name in its place.)

Ask my mother what we're having for lunch. (In this sentence, "mother" describes someone but is not used as a name.)

Geographic Names

Capitalize geographic names that are either proper nouns or proper adjectives.

Planets and heavenly bodies . . . . **Earth, Jupiter, Milky Way**

Continents . . . . **Europe, Asia, South America, Australia, Africa**

Countries . . . . **Chad, Haiti, Greece, Chile, Jordan**

States . . . . **New Mexico, Alabama, West Virginia, Delaware, Iowa**

Provinces . . . . **Alberta, British Columbia, Québec, Ontario**

Cities . . . . **Montreal, Portland**

Counties . . . . **Wayne County, Dade County**

Bodies of water . . . . **Hudson Bay, North Sea, Lake Geneva,**
Saskatchewan River, Indian Ocean, Gulf of Mexico

Landforms . . . . **Appalachian Mountains, Bitterroot Range**

Public areas . . . . **Vietnam Memorial, Sequoia National Forest**

Roads and highways . . . . **New Jersey Turnpike, Interstate 80,**
Central Avenue, Adam's Apple Road

Buildings . . . . **Pentagon, Oriental Theater, Empire State Building**

Titles Used with Names	Capitalize titles used with names of persons. **President Carter** **Dr. Martin Luther King, Jr.** **Mayor Sharon Sayles-Belton** **TIP:** Do not capitalize titles when they are used alone: the president, the doctor, the mayor.
Historical Events	Capitalize the names of historical events, documents, and periods of time. **Boston Tea Party** **Stone Age** **Emancipation Proclamation**
Abbreviations	Capitalize abbreviations of titles and organizations. **M.D.** (doctor of medicine) **ADA** (American Dental Association)
Organizations	Capitalize the name of an organization, an association, or a team and its members. **Girl Scouts of America** **the Democratic Party** **Chicago Bulls** **Republicans**
Titles	Capitalize the first word of a title, the last word, and every word in between except articles (*a, an, the*), short prepositions, and coordinating conjunctions. *National Geographic World* (magazine) **"The Star-Spangled Banner"** (song) *Beauty and the Beast* (movie) *In My Pocket* (book) **TIP:** Don't lowercase every short word in a title. Although *my* is a short word, it is not an article, a preposition, or a coordinating conjunction.
First Words	Capitalize the first word of every sentence. **Our first basketball game is on Monday.** Capitalize the first word of a direct quotation. **Jamir shouted, "Keep that ball moving."**
Days and Months	Capitalize the names of days of the week, months of the year, and holidays. **Wednesday March Easter** **Arbor Day Passover Juneteenth Day** **TIP:** Do not capitalize the seasons. **winter spring summer fall** (or **autumn**)

Names of Religions, Nationalities, Languages	Capitalize the names of religions, nationalities, and languages.

Christianity, Hinduism, Islam (religions)
Australian, Somalian, Chinese (nationalities)
English, Spanish, Hebrew (languages)

Official Names	Capitalize the names of businesses and the official names of their products. (These are called trade names.)

Budget Mart   **Crispy Crunch cereal**
Choconut candy   **Smile toothpaste**

TIP: Do not capitalize a general descriptive word like *toothpaste* when it follows the product name.

Capitalize	Do Not Capitalize
January, March	winter, spring
Grandpa (as a name)	my grandpa (describing him)
Mayor Sayles-Belton	Ms. Sayles-Belton, the mayor
President Washington	George Washington, our first president
Ida B. Wells Elementary School	the local elementary school
Lake Ontario	the lake area
the South (section of the country)	south (a direction)
planet Earth	the earth we live on

Plurals

Nouns Ending in a Consonant	Form the plurals of most nouns by adding *s*.

balloon → balloons   shoe → shoes

Form the plurals of nouns ending in *sh, ch, x, s,* and *z* by adding *es* to the singular.

brush → brushes   buzz → buzzes   bunch → bunches
box → boxes   dress → dresses

Nouns Endings in *o*	Form the plurals of most nouns ending in *o* by adding *s*.

patio → patios   rodeo → rodeos

Form the plurals of most nouns ending in *o*, with a consonant letter just before the *o*, by adding *es*.

echo → echoes   hero → heroes

Except: Musical terms and nouns of Spanish origin form plurals by adding *s*; check your dictionary for other words of this type.

piano → pianos   solo → solos
taco → tacos   burrito → burritos

Nouns Ending in *ful*	Form the plurals of nouns that end with *ful* by adding an *s* at the end of the word. **two spoonfuls** **three tankfuls** **four bowlfuls** **five cupfuls**

Nouns Ending in *f* or *fe*	Form the plurals of nouns that end in *f* or *fe* in one of two ways.
	
	1. If the final *f* is still heard in the plural form of the word, simply add s.
	
	   goof → goofs **chief → chiefs** **safe → safes**
	
	2. If the final *f* has the sound of *v* in the plural form, change the *f* to *v* and add *es*.
	
	   calf → calves **loaf → loaves** **knife → knives**

Nouns Ending in *y*	Form the plurals of common nouns that end in *y* (when a consonant letter comes just before the *y*) by changing the *y* to *i* and adding *es*.
	
	   sky → skies **bunny → bunnies**
	   story → stories **musky → muskies**
	
	Form the plurals of nouns that end in *y* (when a vowel comes before the *y*) by adding only s.
	
	   donkey → donkeys **monkey → monkeys**
	   key → keys **day → days**
	
	Form the plurals of proper nouns that end in *y* by adding only *s*.
	
	Two Penny Candys are opening in our city.

Irregular Nouns	Some nouns form plurals by taking on an irregular spelling.
	
	   child → children **goose → geese**
	   man → men **woman → women**
	   foot → feet **tooth → teeth**
	   ox → oxen **mouse → mice**
	   cactus → cacti or cactuses

Adding an *s*	The plurals of symbols, letters, numerals, and words discussed as words are formed by adding an *apostrophe* and s.
	
	   two ?'s and two !'s **five 7's**
	   ***x*'s and *y*'s** ***a*'s and *an*'s**
	
	TIP: For information on forming plurals and plural possessives, see page 145.

© Great Source. Copying is prohibited.

An **abbreviation** is the shortened form of a word or phrase.

Common Abbreviations	Most abbreviations begin with a capital letter and end with a period.

TIP: The following abbreviations are always acceptable in both formal and informal writing:

Mr.   Mrs.   Ms.   Dr.   Jr.
M.D.   B.C.E.   C.E.   a.m.   p.m. (A.M., P.M.)

In formal writing, do not abbreviate the names of states, countries, months, days, or units of measure. Also do not use signs or symbols (%, &) in place of words.

Acronyms	An acronym is a word formed from the first letter or letters of words in a phrase. Acronyms do not end with a period.

SADD (**S**tudents **A**gainst **D**estructive **D**ecisions)

PIN (**p**ersonal **i**dentification **n**umber)

radar (**ra**dio **d**etecting **a**nd **r**anging)

Initialisms	An initialism is like an acronym except the letters that form the abbreviation are pronounced individually.

TV (television)   **PSA** (public service announcement)

CD (compact disc)   **ASAP** (as soon as possible)

State Abbreviations

	Standard	Postal		Standard	Postal		Standard	Postal
Alabama	**Ala.**	**AL**	Kentucky	**Ky.**	**KY**	North Dakota	**N.D.**	**ND**
Alaska	**Alaska**	**AK**	Louisiana	**La.**	**LA**	Ohio	**Ohio**	**OH**
Arizona	**Ariz.**	**AZ**	Maine	**Maine**	**ME**	Oklahoma	**Okla.**	**OK**
Arkansas	**Ark.**	**AR**	Maryland	**Md.**	**MD**	Oregon	**Ore.**	**OR**
California	**Calif.**	**CA**	Massachusetts	**Mass.**	**MA**	Pennsylvania	**Pa.**	**PA**
Colorado	**Colo.**	**CO**	Michigan	**Mich.**	**MI**	Rhode Island	**R.I.**	**RI**
Connecticut	**Conn.**	**CT**	Minnesota	**Minn.**	**MN**	South Carolina	**S.C.**	**SC**
Delaware	**Del.**	**DE**	Mississippi	**Miss.**	**MS**	South Dakota	**S.D.**	**SD**
District of			Missouri	**Mo.**	**MO**	Tennessee	**Tenn.**	**TN**
Columbia	**D.C.**	**DC**	Montana	**Mont.**	**MT**	Texas	**Tex.**	**TX**
Florida	**Fla.**	**FL**	Nebraska	**Neb.**	**NE**	Utah	**Utah**	**UT**
Georgia	**Ga.**	**GA**	Nevada	**Nev.**	**NV**	Vermont	**Vt.**	**VT**
Hawaii	**Hawaii**	**HI**	New			Virginia	**Va.**	**VA**
Idaho	**Idaho**	**ID**	Hampshire	**N.H.**	**NH**	Washington	**Wash.**	**WA**
Illinois	**Ill.**	**IL**	New Jersey	**N.J.**	**NJ**	West Virginia	**W. Va.**	**WV**
Indiana	**Ind.**	**IN**	New Mexico	**N.M.**	**NM**	Wisconsin	**Wis.**	**WI**
Iowa	**Iowa**	**IA**	New York	**N.Y.**	**NY**	Wyoming	**Wyo.**	**WY**
Kansas	**Kan.**	**KS**	North Carolina	**N.C.**	**NC**			

Checking Your Spelling

A

about
above
absent
accept
accident
accompany
accurate
ache
achieve
across
actual
address
adventure
advertisement
advise
afraid
after
against
agreement
allowance
all right
almost
alone
along
a lot
already
although
always
American
among
amount
ancient
angel
angle
animal
anniversary
anonymous

another
answer
anybody
apartment
apologize
application
appreciate
April
aren't
argument
arithmetic
around
arrival
article
artificial
athlete
athletic
attention
attitude
attractive
audience
August
aunt
author
automobile
autumn
avenue
awful
awhile

B

baggage
balloon
banana
bargain
basement
beautiful
because

become
been
before
beginning
behind
believe
belong
between
bicycle
birthday
biscuit
blanket
blizzard
bought
breakfast
brilliant
brother
brought
bruise
buckle
building
built
burglar
business
busy
button
buy

C

cafeteria
calendar
called
campaign
candidate
canoe
canyon
captain
careful

careless
casserole
caterpillar
caught
celebration
cemetery
century
certain
certificate
change
character
chief
children
chimney
chocolate
choir
choose
Christmas
church
city
civilization
classmates
classroom
climate
closet
cocoa
cocoon
color
come
coming
committee
community
company
complete
concert
congratulate
cooperate
cough
could

couldn't
country
courage
courteous
courtesy
cousin
criticize
cupboard
curious
customer

D

dairy
dangerous
daughter
day
dear
December
decorate
definition
delicious
describe
desert
dessert
developed
didn't
different
difficulty
disappear
disastrous
discover
discussion
distance
divide
division
doctor
does
done
doubt

E

early
earth
Easter
easy
edge
either
electricity
elephant
emergency
encourage
enormous
enough
entertain
environment
every
everybody
exactly
excellent
exercise
exhausted
expensive
experience
explain
expression
eyes

F

face
familiar
family
famous
fashion
faucet
favorite
February
fierce
fifty
finally
first

football
foreign
forty
forward
found
fountain
fourth
fragile
Friday
friend
from
front
fuel
full

G

gadget
generally
generous
genius
gentle
geography
getting
goes
gone
government
grade
graduation
grammar
grateful
great
grocery
group
guarantee
guard
guardian
guess
gymnasium

H

half
handkerchief
handsome
happened
happiness
haven't
having
hazardous
heard
heavy
height
history
holiday
honor
horrible
hospital
hour
humorous
hundreds

I

icicle
ideal
identical
imagine
immediately
immigrant
impatient
important
impossible
incredible
independent
individual
influence
innocent
instead
intelligent
interested
island

J

January
jewelry
journal
journey
judgment
juicy
July
June

K

kitchen
knew
knife
knives
know
knowledge

L

language
laughed
league
leave
length
lesson
letter
light
lightning
likely
listen
literature
little
loose
lovable

M

magazine
making
manufacture
many
March
marriage
material
mathematics
May
maybe
mayor
might
millions
minute
mirror
Monday
money
morning
mountain
music
musician
mysterious

N

natural
necessary
neighborhood
neither
never
nice
noisy
none
no one
nothing
November
nuclear
number

O

obey
occasion
o'clock
October
office
often
once
operate
opposite
other
outside
own

P

package
paragraph
parallel
party
pasture
patience
peace
people
picture

piece
place
played
pleasant
please
pleasure
point
poison
practice
prejudice
preparation
present
president
pretty
principal
privilege
problem
products
psychology
pumpkin

Q

quarter
quickly
quiet
quit
quite
quotient

R

raise
ready
really
reason
receive
recognize
remember
responsibilities
restaurant
right

rough
route

S

safety
said
salad
salary
sandwich
Santa Claus
Saturday
says
scared
scene
school
sentence
September
several
shoes
should
since
skiing
something
sometimes
soon
special
started
store
straight
studying
suddenly
sugar
summer
Sunday
suppose
sure
surprise
surround
swimming
system

T

table
teacher
tear
temperature
terrible
Thanksgiving
their
there
they're
though
thought
thousands
through
Thursday
tired
together
tomorrow
tonight
toys
traveling
trouble
truly
Tuesday
turn

U

unconscious
unfortunately
until
unusual
upon
use
usually

V

vacation
vacuum
vegetable

vehicle
very
violence
visitor
voice
volume

W

wasn't
weather
Wednesday
weight
weird
welcome
welfare
were
we're
what
when
where
which
while
whole
whose
women
world
wouldn't
write
writing
wrote

Y

yellow
yesterday
young
your
you're
yourself

Using the Right Word

You need to use "the right words" in your writing and speaking, and this section will help you do that. First, look over the commonly misused words on this page and the next 7 pages. Then, whenever you have a question about which word is the right word, come back to this section for help. (Remember to look for your word in a dictionary if you don't find it here.)

a, an	**I played a joke on my dad.** (Use *a* before words beginning with a consonant sound.) **I placed an ugly rubber chicken under his pillow.** (Use *an* before words beginning with a vowel sound.)
accept, except	**Please accept my apology.** (*Accept* means "to receive.") **Everyone except me finished the race.** (*Except* means "other than.")
allowed, aloud	**We are allowed to read to partners in class.** (*Allowed* means "permitted.") **We may not read aloud in the library, however.** (*Aloud* is an adverb meaning "clearly heard.")
a lot	**A lot of my friends like jeans with holes in them.** (*A lot* is always two words.)
already, all ready	**I already finished my homework.** (*Already* is an adverb telling when.) **Now I'm all ready to shoot some hoops.** (*All ready* is a phrase meaning "completely ready.")
ant, aunt	**An ant is an insect.** **An aunt is a close relative.**
ate, eight	**I ate a bowl of popcorn.** **He had eight pieces of licorice.**
bare, bear	**She put her bare feet into the cool stream.** **She didn't see the bear fishing on the other side.**
blew, blue	**I blew on my cold hands.** **The tips of my fingers looked almost blue.**
board, bored	**A board is a piece of wood.** **You feel bored when there's nothing to do.**

brake, break	Pump the brake to slow down.
	You don't want to break a bone.
bring, take	Please bring me my glasses.
	(*Bring* means "to move toward the speaker.")
	Take your dishes to the kitchen.
	(*Take* means "to carry away.")
by, buy	Did a hawk just fly by my window?
	I better buy some new glasses.
can, may	Can I go off the high dive?
	(I am asking if I have the "ability" to do it.)
	May I go off the high dive?
	(I am asking for "permission" to do something.)
capital, capitol	The capital city of Texas is Austin.
	Be sure to begin Austin with a capital letter.
	My uncle works in the capitol building.
	(*Capitol*, with an "ol," is used when writing about a government building.)
cents, scent, sent	Each rose costs 99 cents.
	The scent (smell) of the flowers is sweet.
	Dad sent Mom a dozen roses.
chose, choose	David chose to take drum lessons last year.
	He will choose a different instrument this year.
	(*Chose* [chōz] is the past tense of the verb *choose* [chooz].)
close, clothes	Close the window.
	Then put the clothes in the dryer.
coarse, course	A cat's tongue feels coarse, like sandpaper.
	I took a course called "Caring for Cats."
creak, creek	Old houses creak when the wind blows hard.
	The water in the nearby creek is clear and cold.
dear, deer	Amber is my dear friend.
	The deer enjoyed the sweet corn in her garden.
desert, dessert	Cactuses grow in the desert.
	My favorite dessert is strawberry pie.

dew, do, **due**	The dew on the grass got my new shoes wet. I do my homework right after school. The report is due on Wednesday.
die, dye	The plant will die if it isn't watered. I want to dye my hair bright orange.
doesn't, **don't**	She doesn't like green bananas. (**doesn't** = does not) I don't either. (**don't** = do not)
fewer, less	We had fewer snow days this winter. (*Fewer* refers to something you can count.) That meant less time for ice-skating. (*Less* refers to something you cannot count.)
find, fined	Did you find your book? Yes, but I was fined because it was overdue.
fir, fur	Fir trees are evergreen trees. Polar bears have thick fur coats.
for, four	You may eat the kiwis for a snack. The four of you may also share the crackers.
good, well	Ling looks good in that outfit. (*Good* is an adjective modifying "Ling.") It fits her well. (*Well* is an adverb modifying "fits.")
hare, hair	A hare looks like a large rabbit. My hair looks like a wet rabbit.
heal, heel	It takes a long time for a blister to heal. Gracie has a blister on her heel.
hear, here	I couldn't hear your directions. I was over here, and you were way over there.
heard, herd	We heard the noise, all right! It sounded like a herd of charging elephants.
heir, air	An heir is a person who inherits something. Air is what we breathe.

hi, high	Say hi to the pilot for me.
	How high is this plane flying?
hole, whole	A donut has a hole in the middle of it.
	Montel ate a whole donut.
hour, our	It takes one hour to ride to the beach.
	Let's pack our lunches and go.
its, it's	This backpack is no good; its zipper is stuck.
	(*Its* shows possession.)
	It's also ripped.
	(*It's* is the contraction of "it is.")
knew, new	I knew it was going to rain.
	I still wanted to wear my new shoes.
knight, night	The knight stood guard by the iron gates.
	Torches were lit for the long night.
knot, not	I have a knot in my shoelaces.
	I am not able to untie the tangled mess.
know, no	Do you know all the dates for our history test?
	No, let's study them together.
knows, nose	Mr. Beck knows at least a billion historical facts.
	His nose is always in a book.
lay, lie	Just lay the sleeping bags on the floor.
	(*Lay* means "to place.")
	After the hike, we'll lie down and rest.
	(*Lie* means "to recline.")
lead, led	Some old paint contains lead.
	I get to lead the ponies around the showring.
	Yesterday the drill team led the parade past the arena.
learn, teach	I need to learn these facts about the moon.
	(*Learn* means "to get information.")
	Tomorrow I have to teach the science lesson.
	(*Teach* means "to give information.")

loose, lose	Lee's pet tarantula is loose! (*Loose* [lo͞os] means "free or untied.") **No one but Lee could lose a big, fat spider.** (*Lose* [lo͞oz] means "to misplace or fail to win.")
made, maid	Yes, I have made a big mess. I need a maid to help me clean it up.
mail, male	Many people receive mail on their computers. Men are male; women are female.
meat, meet	I think meat can be a part of a healthful diet. We were so excited to meet the senator.
metal, medal	Gold is a precious metal. Is the Olympic first-place medal actually made of gold?
miners, minors	Some coal miners suffer from black lung disease. Minors are young people who are not legally adults.
oar, or, ore	You use an oar to row a boat. Either Kim or Makaila will do the rowing. Iron ore is a mineral.
one, won	Markus bought one raffle ticket. He won the bike with that single ticket.
pain, pane	Cuts, bruises, and broken bones cause pain. I can finally see through the pane of clean glass.
pair, pare, pear	A pair (two) of pigeons roosted on our windowsill. To pare an apple means to peel it. A ripe pear is sweet and juicy.
passed, past	The school bus passed a stalled truck. In the past, most children walked to school.
peace, piece	Ms. Brown likes peace and quiet in her room. I like a piece of cake in my lunch.
plain, plane	Toni wanted a plain (basic) white dress. The coyote ran across the flat plain. A stunt plane can fly upside down.

pore, pour, poor	A pore is a tiny opening in the skin. Please pour me another glass of juice. Rich is the opposite of poor.
principal, principle	**Our** principal **is a strong leader.** (The noun *principal* is a school administrator; the adjective *principal* means "most important.") **She asks students to follow this** principle: **Respect each other, and I'll respect you.** (*Principle* means "idea" or "belief.")
quiet, quit, quite	**Libraries should be** quiet **places.** Quit **talking, please.** **I hear** quite **a bit of whispering going on.**
raise, rays, raze	**Please don't** raise (lift) **the shades.** **The sun's** rays **are very bright this afternoon.** **To** raze **means "to tear something down."**
read, red	**Have you** read **any books by Betsy Byars?** **Why are most barns painted** red?
right, write, rite	**Is this the** right (correct) **place to turn right?** **I'll** write **the directions on a note card.** **The pastor performed the marriage** rite (ceremony).
road, rode, rowed	**My house is one block from the main** road. **I** rode **my bike to the pond.** **Then I** rowed **the boat to my favorite fishing spot.**
scene, seen	**The movie has a great chase** scene. **Have you** seen **it yet?**
sea, see	**A** sea **is a body of salty water.** **I** see **a tall ship on the horizon.**
seam, seem	**The** seam **in my jacket is ripped.** **I** seem **to always catch my sleeve on the door handle.**
sew, so, sow	**Shauna loves to** sew **her own clothes.** **She saves her allowance,** so **she can buy fabric.** **I'd rather** sow **seeds and watch my garden grow.**

sit, set	May I sit on one of those folding chairs?
	Yes, if you help me set them up first.
some, sum	I have some math problems to do.
	What is the sum of 58 + 17?
son, sun	Joe Jackson is the son of Kate Jackson.
	The sun is the source of the earth's energy.
sore, soar	Our feet and legs were sore after the long hike.
	We watched hawks soar above us.
stationery, stationary	Wu designs his own stationery (paper) on the computer.
	A stationary bike stays in place while you pedal it.
steal, steel	You can steal third base, but don't take it home!
	Many knives are made of steel.
tail, tale	A snake uses its tail to move its body.
	"Sammy the Spotted Snake" is my favorite tall tale.
than, then	Jana's card collection is bigger than Erica's.
	(*Than* is used in a comparison.)
	When Jana is finished, then we can play.
	(*Then* tells when.)
their, there, they're	What should we do with their cards?
	(*Their* shows ownership.)
	Put them over there for now.
	They're going to pick them up later.
	(they're = they are)
threw, through	He threw the ball at the basket.
	It swished through the net.
to, too, two	Josie passed the ball to Shannon.
	Lea was too tired to guard her.
	(*Too* means "very.")
	The fans jumped and cheered, too.
	(*Too* means "also.")
	Maria easily scored two points.
waist, waste	My little sister's waist is tiny.
	No part of the buffalo went to waste.

wait, weight	I can't wait for the field trip.
	My brother lifts weights to get strong.
way, weigh	Show me the way to the gym.
	Birds weigh very little because of their hollow bones.
weak, week	The opposite of strong is weak.
	There are seven days in a week.
wear, where	The crossing guards wear yellow ponchos.
	Where do you think they got them?
weather, whether	I like rainy weather.
	My dad goes golfing whether it's nice out or not.
which, witch	Which book should I read?
	You'll like *The Lion, the Witch, and the Wardrobe*.
who, which, that	The man who answered the door was my dad.
	The movie, which was very funny, ended too soon.
	The puppy that I really wanted was sold already.
who, whom	Who ordered this pizza?
	The pizza was ordered by whom?
who's, whose	Who's that knocking at the door? (who's = who is)
	Whose door are you talking about?
wood, would	Some baseball bats are made of wood.
	Would you like to play baseball after school?
you're, your	You're talking to the right person! (you're = you are)
	You can pick up your pizzas after school.

Understanding Sentences

PARTS OF A SENTENCE

A **sentence** has two basic parts—the subject and the predicate. The subject usually tells who or what is doing something. The predicate expresses action or links the subject to another part of the sentence.

Subject

A **subject** is the part of a sentence that does something.

> Marisha **baked a chocolate cake.**

A subject can also be the word that is talked about.

> She **is a marvelous cook.**

Simple Subject

A simple subject is the subject without the words that describe it.

> **Marisha's little** sister **likes to help.**

Complete Subject

The complete subject is the simple subject and all the words that describe it.

> Marisha's little sister **likes to help.**
>
> ("Marisha's little sister" is the complete subject.)

Compound Subject

A compound subject has two or more simple subjects.

> Marisha **and her** sister **frosted the cake.**

Predicate

A **predicate** (verb) is the part of the sentence that says something about the subject.

> Marisha baked **the cake for my birthday.**
>
> ("Baked" tells what the subject did.)

Simple Predicate

A simple predicate (verb) is the predicate without the words that modify or complete it.

> Marisha baked **the cake yesterday.**

Complete Predicate

The complete predicate is the simple predicate with all the words that modify or complete it.

> Marisha baked the cake yesterday.
>
> (The complete predicate is "baked the cake yesterday.")

Compound Predicate

A compound predicate has two or more simple predicates.

> She decorated **it and** hid **it in the cupboard.**

Clauses

A **clause** is a group of words that has a subject and a predicate. A clause can be independent or dependent.

Independent Clauses

An independent clause expresses a complete thought and can stand alone as a sentence.

I ride my bike to school

Dependent Clauses

A dependent clause does not express a complete thought and cannot stand alone as a sentence. Dependent clauses usually begin with a subordinating conjunction like *when*. (See page 183.)

when **the weather is nice**

TIP: Some dependent clauses begin with a relative pronoun like *who* or *that*. (See page 175.)

An independent clause plus a dependent clause form a complex sentence.

I ride my bike to school when the weather is nice.

Phrases

A **phrase** is a group of related words. Phrases cannot stand alone as sentences.

Noun Phrase

This is a noun phrase. It lacks a predicate.

the student

Verb Phrase

This is a verb phrase. It lacks a subject.

wrote a report

Prepositional Phrase

This is a prepositional phrase. (See page 182.)

about George Washington

Appositive Phrase

This is an appositive phrase.

our first president

Note: When you put these phrases together, they become a sentence.

The student wrote a report about George Washington, our first president.

TYPES OF SENTENCES

Simple Sentences	A simple sentence has only one independent clause (and states only one complete thought). However, it may have a compound subject, compound predicate—or both—and still be a simple sentence. **My** knees ache. (Simple subject, simple predicate) Cory **and** I skated **for two hours.** (Compound subject, simple predicate) **My** face **and** neck look **red and** feel **hot.** (Compound subject, compound predicate)
Compound Sentences	A compound sentence is made up of two or more simple sentences joined by a comma and a coordinating conjunction (*and, but, or*), or by a semicolon. (See page 183 for more about coordinating conjunctions.) **I've skated in Los Angeles,** but **I have only seen a picture of New York.** (The conjunction "but" connects two independent clauses.) **Los Angeles is 30 miles from my home; New York is 3,000 miles away.** (A semicolon connects two independent clauses.)
Complex Sentences	A complex sentence contains one independent clause (in **black**) and one or more dependent clauses (in color). Dependent clauses begin with a subordinating conjunction like *because* or a relative pronoun like *who* or *that*. Because it was raining, **the game was called off.** **The students,** who were wet and cold, **got back on the bus.**

KINDS OF SENTENCES

Declarative Sentences	Declarative sentences make statements. They tell something about a person, a place, a thing, or an idea. **The capital of Florida is Tallahassee.**
Interrogative Sentences	Interrogative sentences ask questions. **Did you know that Florida's major industry is tourism?**
Imperative Sentences	Imperative sentences give commands. **You must never swim alone.** **TIP:** Imperative sentences often use an understood subject (you). **Never swim alone. Stay here.**
Exclamatory Sentences	Exclamatory sentences communicate strong emotion or surprise. **Watch out for sharks!**

SENTENCE PROBLEMS

Sentence Fragments

A **sentence fragment** is a group of words that only looks like a sentence. It does not express a complete thought because important information is missing.

Incorrect: **Thinks roller coasters are cool.**
(The subject is missing.)

Correct: **Martina thinks roller coasters are cool.**

Incorrect: **Not my favorite type of ride.**
(The subject and verb are both missing.)

Correct: **Roller coasters are not my favorite type of ride.**

Run-On Sentences

A **run-on sentence** happens when two sentences are joined without punctuation or a connecting word.

Incorrect: **The evening was warm it was time to catch fireflies.**
(Punctuation is needed.)

Correct: **The evening was warm. It was time to catch fireflies.** (A period has been added, and a letter has been capitalized.)

Correct: **The evening was warm, and it was time to catch fireflies.** (A comma and the conjunction "and" have been added.)

Rambling Sentences

A **rambling sentence** occurs when you put too many short sentences together with the word *and*.

Incorrect: **I went skating down at the pond and three kids from my school were there and we fell on our fannies again and again and we laughed so much our stomachs hurt!** (Too many *and*'s are used.)

Correct: **I went skating down at the pond, and three kids from my school were there. We fell on our fannies again and again. We laughed so much our stomachs hurt!**

Double Subjects

Do not use a pronoun immediately after the subject. The result is usually a double subject.

Incorrect: **Some cats they eat all the time.**
(The pronoun "they" should be omitted.)

Correct: **Some cats eat all the time.**

Confusing "Of" for "Have"

Do not use *of* in a sentence when you really mean *have*. (When *have* is said quickly, it sometimes sounds like *of*.)

Incorrect: **We should of brought an umbrella.**

Correct: **We should have brought an umbrella.**

Pronoun-Antecedent Agreement	Make sure the pronouns in your sentences agree with the words they replace, which are called antecedents. Incorrect: **If Carlo and his friends each eat three double cheeseburgers, he will be overstuffed.** (The pronoun "he" is singular. The antecedents "Carlo and his friends" are plural.) Correct: **If Carlo and his friends each eat three double cheeseburgers, they will be overstuffed.** (Now the pronoun and its antecedents agree; they are plural.)
Double Negatives	Do not use two negative words, like *never* and *no* or *not* and *no*, in the same sentence. Incorrect: **Never give no one a note during class.** Correct: **Never give anyone a note during class.** Incorrect: **I didn't have no mistakes in my paragraph.** Correct: **I didn't have any mistakes in my paragraph.**

SENTENCE AGREEMENT

	Make sure that the subjects and verbs in your sentences agree with each other. If you use a singular subject, use a singular verb; if you use a plural subject, use a plural verb.
One Subject	Most basic sentences have one subject followed by the verb. **Amy wants to go bowling.** ("Amy" and "wants" agree because they are both singular.) **Her parents want to go bowling, too.** ("Parents" and "want" agree because they are both plural.)
Compound Subjects Connected by "And"	If a sentence contains a compound subject connected by *and*, it needs a plural verb. **Harry and Emil spend time playing tennis.** **Sarah and Maria join them.**
Compound Subjects Connected by "Or"	If a sentence contains a compound subject connected by *or*, the verb must agree with the subject nearer to it. **Either the cat or the dog pounces on me each morning.** (A singular verb, "pounces," is needed because "dog" is singular.) **Anna or her brothers feed the pets each evening.** (A plural verb, "feed," is needed because "brothers" is plural.) ***Helpful Hint:*** Sometimes the subject will not come before the verb. This happens in sentences beginning with the word *there* (There are two dogs) and in questions (Is this dog yours?).

COMBINING WITH KEY WORDS

Key Word

Ideas included in short sentences can be combined by moving a key word from one sentence to the other.

Two Sentences:

Kelly's necklace sparkles. It is beaded.

Combined with an Adjective:

Kelly's beaded necklace sparkles.

Two Sentences:

I am going to a sleepover. I'm going tomorrow.

Combined with an Adverb:

Tomorrow I am going to a sleepover.

Series of Words

Ideas included in short sentences can be combined into one sentence using a series of words.

Short Sentences:

My teacher is strict. My teacher is organized. My teacher is fair.

Combined with a Series of Words:

My teacher is strict, organized, and fair.

Phrases

Ideas from short sentences can be combined into one sentence using phrases. (See page 166.)

Two Sentences:

Our cat curls up. He curls up on top of my homework.

Combined with a Prepositional Phrase:

Our cat curls up on top of my homework.

Two Sentences:
Mrs. Keller makes great cookies.
Mrs. Keller is our next-door neighbor.

Combined with an Appositive Phrase:

Mrs. Keller, our next-door neighbor, makes great cookies.

Compound Subjects and Verbs

A compound subject is two or more subjects connected by a conjunction. A compound verb is two or more verbs connected by a conjunction.

Two Sentences:

Tory danced around the room. Mary danced around the room, too.

Combined with a Compound Subject:

Tory and Mary danced around the room.

Two Sentences:

Jon skated onto the pond. He made a perfect figure eight.

Combined with a Compound Verb:

Jon skated onto the pond and made a perfect figure eight.

COMBINING WITH LONGER SENTENCES

Coordinating Conjunctions

A compound sentence is made up of two or more simple sentences joined together. The conjunctions *and, but, or, nor, for, so,* and *yet* are used to connect the simple sentences. (Place a comma before the conjunction.)

Two Sentences:

My puppy has hair over her eyes. She looks like a dust mop.

Combined with "And":

My puppy has hair over her eyes, and she looks like a dust mop.

Two Sentences:

Our dog chews shoes. He won't touch my smelly slippers.

Combined with "But":

Our dog chews shoes, but he won't touch my smelly slippers.

Subordinating Conjunctions

A complex sentence is made up of two ideas connected by a subordinating conjunction (*because, when, since, after, before,* etc.) or by a relative pronoun (*who, whose, which,* and *that*).

Two Sentences:

My friend shares his lunch with me.
He doesn't like what his dad packs.

Combined with "Because":

My friend shares his lunch with me because he doesn't like what his dad packs.

Two Sentences:

Very cold weather closed school for a day.
The cold weather came down from Canada.

Combined with "Which":

Very cold weather, which came down from Canada, closed school for a day.

Parts of Speech

NOUNS

A **noun** is a word that names a person, a place, a thing, or an idea.

Person:	**Nadia, friend, Josh, parent**
Place:	**home, Miami, city, backyard**
Thing:	**baseball, homework, secret**
Idea:	**happiness, trouble, friendship**

Kinds of Nouns

Common Nouns

A common noun is any noun that does not name a specific person, place, thing, or idea. Common nouns are not capitalized.

man   park   team   holiday

Proper Nouns

A proper noun names a specific person, place, thing, or idea. Proper nouns are capitalized.

Reggie White   Lincoln Park   Lakers   Labor Day

Concrete Nouns

A concrete noun names a thing that can be seen or touched. Concrete nouns are either common or proper.

magazine   cactus   Washington Monument

Abstract Nouns

An abstract noun names something that cannot be seen or touched. Abstract nouns are either common or proper.

love   democracy   Christianity   Judaism

Number of Nouns

Singular Nouns

A singular noun names one person, place, thing, or idea.

room   paper   pen pal   hope

Plural Nouns

A plural noun names more than one person, place, thing, or idea.

rooms   papers   pen pals   hopes

Uses of Nouns

Subject Nouns

A noun may be the subject of a sentence. The subject is the part of the sentence that does something or is being talked about.

Joe **gave Nadia a note.**

(The noun "Joe" did something: "gave Nadia a note.")

Possessive Nouns	A possessive noun shows ownership. Use an apostrophe and *s* to form possessive nouns. (See page 145.) **The** book's **ending is a big surprise.** (The apostrophe and the "s" added to "book" show that the "ending" is part of the book.)
Direct Objects	A noun is a direct object when it receives the action of the verb. **Nadia read the** book. ("Book" is the direct object because it receives the action of the verb "read.")
Indirect Objects	A noun is an indirect object when it names the person to whom or for whom something is done. **Joe gave** Nadia **the book.** (The book is given *to whom*? The book is given to "Nadia," the indirect object.)
Objects of a Preposition	A noun is an object of a preposition when it is part of a prepositional phrase. (See page 182.) **Nadia put the book on the** shelf. (The noun "shelf" is the object of the preposition "on.")

Parts of Speech

Nouns	Words that name a person, a place, a thing, or an idea. *(Bill, office, billboard, confusion)*
Pronouns	Words used in place of nouns. *(I, me, her, them, who, which, those, myself, some)*
Verbs	Words that express action or state of being. *(is, are, run, jump)*
Adjectives	Words that describe a noun or pronoun. *(tall, quiet, three, the, neat)*
Adverbs	Words that describe a verb, an adjective, or another adverb. *(gently, easily, fast, very)*
Interjections	Words (set off by commas or exclamation points) that show emotion or surprise. *(Wow, Oh, Yikes!)*
Prepositions	Words that show position or direction and introduce prepositional phrases. *(on, near, over, on top of)*
Conjunctions	Words that connect words or groups of words. *(and, or, because)*

A **pronoun** is a word used in place of a noun.

Carlotta rescued an injured sandpiper.

She took it to a veterinarian.

("She" is a pronoun that replaces the noun "Carlotta." "It" is a pronoun that replaces the noun "sandpiper.")

Antecedents

An antecedent is the noun that a pronoun refers to or replaces. All pronouns have antecedents.

Anju's skateboard glides easily now that it is oiled.

("Skateboard" is the antecedent of the pronoun "it.")

The pronouns in your sentences must agree with their antecedents in number and person.

Anju's skateboard works great now that it is oiled.

(The pronoun "it" and its antecedent "skateboard" are both singular, so they agree.)

The other kids' boards look like they could use some oil, too.

(The pronoun "they" and its antecedent "boards" are both plural, so they agree.)

Number of Pronouns

Pronouns can be either singular or plural.

I flipped a skateboard.   We flipped the skateboards.

Personal Pronouns

Singular: **I, me, you, he, she, him, her, it, my, mine, your, yours, his, hers, its**

Plural: **we, us, you, they, them, our, ours, your, yours, their, theirs**

Note: My, your, our, its and *their* come before nouns and function as possessive adjectives. Other pronouns such as *his* or *her* may or may not come before nouns.

Uses of Pronouns

A subject pronoun is used as the subject of a sentence.

I can tell jokes well.

They really make people laugh.

Singular: **I, you, he, she, it**

Plural: **we, you, they**

Object Pronouns

An object pronoun is used as a direct object, as an indirect object, or as the object of a preposition.

> **Mr. Otto encourages** me. ("Me," a direct object, receives the action of the verb "encourages.")
>
> **Mr. Otto often gives** us **extra help with math.** ("Us," an indirect object, names the people for whom something is done.)
>
> **My friends made a funny card for** him. ("Him" is the object in the prepositional phrase "for him.")

> Singular: **me, you, him, her, it**
> Plural: **us, you, them**

Possessive Pronouns

A possessive pronoun shows ownership. It can be used before a noun, or it can stand alone.

> **Gloria finished writing** her **story.** ("Her" comes before the noun "story.")
>
> **The idea for the plot was** mine. ("Mine" can stand alone.)

> Before a noun: **my, your, his, her, its, our, their**
> Stand alone: **mine, yours, his, hers, its, ours, theirs**

Other Pronouns

Relative Pronouns

A relative pronoun connects one part of a sentence with a word in another part of the sentence.

> **Any fifth grader** who **wants to join our music group should see Carlos.**

Indefinite Pronouns

An indefinite pronoun refers to people or things that are not named or known.

> Nobody **is here to videotape the practice.**

Types of Pronouns

Relative
who, whom, whose, which, what, that, whoever, whatever, whichever

Indefinite

all	both	everything	nobody	several
another	each	few	none	some
any	each one	many	no one	somebody
anybody	either	most	nothing	someone
anyone	everybody	much	one	something
anything	everyone	neither	other	such

VERBS

A **verb** shows action or links the subject to another word in the sentence. The verb is the main word in the predicate part of the sentence.

The boys hike **along the river.** (The verb "hike" shows action.)

I am **happy about that.**
(The verb "am" links the subject "I" to the word "happy.")

Kinds of Verbs

Action Verbs

An action verb tells what the subject is doing.

I usually watch **the entire game.**

Sometimes I leave **after the third quarter.**

Linking Verbs

A linking verb links a subject to a noun or an adjective in the predicate part of the sentence.

That car is **a convertible.**
(The verb "is" links the subject "car" to the noun "convertible.")

My new car looks **shiny.**
(The verb "looks" links the subject "car" to the adjective "shiny.")

> The most common linking verbs are forms of the verb *be:*
>
> **is, are, was, were, am, being, been**
>
> Other linking verbs include the following:
>
> **smell, look, taste, remain, feel, appear, sound, seem, become, grow, stand, turn**

Helping Verbs

Helping verbs (also called auxiliary verbs) include *has, had,* and *have; do* and *did;* and forms of the verb "be" (*is, are, was, were,* etc.).

Lee will **write in his journal.**
(The verb "will" helps state a future action, "will write.")

Lee has been **writing in his journal.**
(The verbs "has" and "been" help state a continuing action, "has been writing.")

> The most common helping verbs are listed below:
>
> **shall, will, should, would, could, must, can, may, have, had, has, do, did**
>
> The forms of the verb "be" are also helping verbs:
>
> **is, are, was, were, am, being, been**

Tenses of Verbs

The time of a verb is called its tense. Tense is shown by endings (talk*ed*), by helping verbs (*did* talk), or by both (*have* talk*ed*).

Present Tense	The present tense of a verb states an action that is *happening now* or that *happens regularly*. **I** like **soccer.** **We** practice **every day.**
Past Tense	The past tense of a verb states an action or state of being that *happened at a specific time in the past*. **Anne** kicked **the soccer ball.** **She** was **the goalie.**
Future Tense	The future tense of a verb states an action that *will take place*. It is formed by using *will* or *shall* before the main verb. **I** will like **soccer forever.** **We** shall practice **every day.**

Forms of Verbs

Singular Verbs	A singular verb is used when the subject in a sentence is singular. **Ben** likes **cream cheese and olive sandwiches.** (The subject "Ben" and the verb "likes" are both singular.)
Plural Verbs	A plural verb is used when the subject is plural. **Black olives** taste **like wax.** (The subject "olives" and the verb "taste" are both plural.) **TIP:** When a subject and verb are both singular or plural, they agree in number. (See page 169.)
Active Verbs	A verb is active if the subject is doing, did, or will do the action. **Kara** threw **a fastball.** ("Threw" is active because the subject "Kara" did the action.)
Passive Verbs	A verb is passive if the subject does not do the action. **A fastball** was thrown **by Kara.** ("Was thrown" is passive because the subject "fastball" is not doing the action.)
Regular Verbs	Most verbs in the English language are regular. Add *ed* to regular verbs to state a past action; use *has, have,* or *had* with the *ed* form to help state some past actions. **I** play.　**Yesterday I** played.　**I** have played. **He** calls.　**Yesterday he** called.　**He** has called.

Irregular Verbs

Some verbs in the English language are irregular. Instead of adding *ed*, the word changes to state a past action. (See the chart below.)

I speak. **Yesterday I** spoke. I have spoken.
She runs. **Yesterday she** ran. **She** has run.

Irregular Forms of Verbs

The principal parts of some common irregular verbs are listed below. The part used with the helping verbs *has, have,* or *had* is called the past participle.

Present Tense	I hide.	She hides.
Past Tense	Yesterday I hid.	Yesterday she hid.
Past Participle	I have hidden.	She has hidden.

Present Tense	Past Tense	Past Participle	Present Tense	Past Tense	Past Participle
am, are	was, were	been	lie (recline)	lay	lain
begin	began	begun	make	made	made
bite	bit	bitten	ride	rode	ridden
blow	blew	blown	ring	rang	rung
break	broke	broken	rise	rose	risen
bring	brought	brought	run	ran	run
burst	burst	burst	see	saw	seen
catch	caught	caught	set	set	set
come	came	come	shake	shook	shaken
dive	dove,		shine (light)	shone	shone
	dived	dived	shrink	shrank	shrunk
do	did	done	sing	sang, sung	sung
draw	drew	drawn	sink	sank, sunk	sunk
drink	drank	drunk	sit	sat	sat
drive	drove	driven	speak	spoke	spoken
eat	ate	eaten	spring	sprang,	
fall	fell	fallen		sprung	sprung
fight	fought	fought	steal	stole	stolen
fly	flew	flown	swear	swore	sworn
freeze	froze	frozen	swim	swam	swum
give	gave	given	swing	swung	swung
go	went	gone	take	took	taken
grow	grew	grown	tear	tore	torn
hang	hung	hung	throw	threw	thrown
hide	hid	hidden, hid	wake	woke	woken
know	knew	known	wear	wore	worn
lay (place)	laid	laid	weave	wove	woven
lead	led	led	write	wrote	written

ADJECTIVES

Adjectives are words that modify (describe) nouns or pronouns. Adjectives tell *what kind, how many,* or *which one.*

> Male peacocks have beautiful feathers.

> The feathers are colorful. (An adjective after a linking verb is called a "predicate adjective.")

Articles

The words *a, an,* and *the* are special adjectives called articles.

> "Owlet" is the name for a baby owl.

Proper Adjectives

Proper adjectives (in color) are formed from proper nouns. They are always capitalized. Common adjectives (in *italics*) are any adjectives that are not proper.

> On a *cold* Wisconsin day, a Hawaiian vacation sounds *wonderful.*

Forms of Adjectives

Positive Adjectives

The positive (base) form of an adjective describes a noun without comparing it to another noun.

> A hummingbird is small.

Comparative Adjectives

The comparative form of an adjective compares two people, places, things, or ideas.

> A hummingbird is smaller than a sparrow.

> (The ending *er* is added to one-syllable adjectives.)

> Hummingbirds are more colorful than sparrows. ("More" is added before most adjectives with two or more syllables.)

Superlative Adjectives

The superlative form of an adjective compares three or more people, places, things, or ideas.

> The hummingbird is the smallest bird I've seen.

> (The ending "est" is added to one-syllable adjectives.)

> The parrot is the most colorful bird in the zoo. ("Most" is added before most adjectives with two or more syllables.)

Irregular Forms of Adjectives

Positive	Comparative	Superlative
good	**better**	**best**
bad	**worse**	**worst**
many	**more**	**most**
little	**less**	**least**

Note: Do not use *more* or *most* with forms of *good* and *bad.*

Special Kinds of Adjectives

Compound Adjectives	Compound adjectives are made up of more than one word. Some compound adjectives are spelled as one word; others are hyphenated. **Many** white-throated **sparrows live in our** evergreen **bushes.**
Two-Syllable Adjectives	Some two-syllable adjectives show comparisons either by their *er*/*est* endings or by modifiers like *more* and *most*. friendly friendlier friendliest friendly more friendly most friendly

ADVERBS

Adverbs are words that modify (describe) verbs, adjectives, or other adverbs. Adverbs tell *how, when, where, how often,* and *how much.*

The softball team practices faithfully.
("Faithfully" modifies the verb "practices.")

Yesterday's practice was extra **long.**
("Extra" modifies the adjective "long.")

Last night the players slept quite **soundly.**
("Quite" modifies the adverb "soundly.")

Types of Adverbs

Adverbs of Time	Adverbs of time tell *when, how often,* or *how long.* **Max batted** first. (when) **Katie's team played** weekly. (how often) **Her team was in first place** briefly. (how long)
Adverbs of Place	Adverbs of place tell *where.* **The first pitch curved** inside. (where) **The batter leaned** forward. (where)
Adverbs of Manner	Adverbs of manner tell *how* something is done. **Max waited** eagerly **for the next pitch.** (how)
Adverbs of Degree	Adverbs of degree tell *how much* or *how little.* **The catcher was** totally **surprised.** (how much) **He** scarcely **saw the fastball coming.** (how little) **TIP:** Adverbs often end in *ly,* but not always. Words like *not, never, very,* and *always* are common adverbs.

Forms of Adverbs

Positive Adverbs	The positive (base) form of an adverb does not make a comparison. **Max plays hard from the first pitch to the last out.**
Comparative Adverbs	The comparative form of an adverb is formed by adding *er* to one-syllable adverbs or the word *more* or *less* before longer adverbs. **He plays harder than his cousin plays.** **He plays more often than his cousin does.**
Superlative Adverbs	The superlative form of an adverb is formed by adding *est* to one-syllable adverbs or the word *most* or *least* before longer adverbs. **Max plays hardest in close games.** **Max plays most often in center field.**

Special Forms of Adverbs

Positive	Comparative	Superlative
well	**better**	**best**
badly	**worse**	**worst**
quickly	**more quickly**	**most quickly**
fairly	**less fairly**	**least fairly**

TIP: Do not confuse *well* and *good*. *Good* is an adjective and *well* is usually an adverb. (See page 159.)

INTERJECTIONS

Interjections are words or phrases that express strong emotion. Commas or exclamation points are used to separate interjections from the rest of the sentence.

Wow, look at those mountains!

Hey! Keep your eyes on the road!

PREPOSITIONS

Prepositions are words that show position or direction and introduce prepositional phrases.

In our house, our cats do what they please.

Object of a Preposition

The object of the preposition is the noun or pronoun that comes after the preposition.

Smacker watches from the desk drawer.

(The noun "drawer" is the object of the preposition "from.")

Then Smacker ducks inside it.

(The pronoun "it" is the object of the preposition "inside." The antecedent of the pronoun "it" is the noun "drawer" in the previous sentence.)

Prepositional Phrases

Prepositional phrases include a preposition, the object of the preposition (a noun or a pronoun), and any words that modify the object.

Jo-jo sneaks toward the gerbil cage.

("Toward" is a preposition, "cage" is the object of the preposition, and "the" and "gerbil" modify "cage.")

Common Prepositions

aboard	below	in	through
about	beneath	inside	throughout
above	beside	into	till
across	besides	like	to
across from	between	near	toward
after	beyond	of	under
against	but	off	underneath
along	by	on	until
along with	down	onto	up
among	during	out	up to
around	except	outside	upon
at	except for	over	with
before	for	past	within
behind	from	since	without

CONJUNCTIONS

Conjunctions connect individual words or groups of words.

The river is wide and deep.

We can fish in the morning or in the evening.

Coordinating Conjunctions

A coordinating conjunction connects equal parts: two or more words, phrases, or clauses.

The river rushes down the valley, and then it winds through the prairie.

(The conjunction "and" connects two independent clauses to make a compound sentence.)

Subordinating Conjunctions

A subordinating conjunction often introduces the dependent clause in a complex sentence.

Our trip was delayed when the snowstorm hit.

We stayed in town until the snow stopped.

Common Conjunctions

Coordinating **and, but, or, nor, for, so, yet**

Subordinating **after, although, as, as if,
as long as, as though, because,
before, if, in order that, since, so,
so that, that, though, unless, until,
when, where, whereas, while**

TIP: Relative pronouns can also connect clauses.
(See page 175.)